STUDIES IN COMMONWEALTH POLITICS AND HISTORY

No. 9

General Editors: Professor W. H. MORRIS-JONES
Institute of Commonwealth Studies
University of London

Professor DENNIS AUSTIN
Department of Government
University of Manchester

FROM RHODESIA TO ZIMBABWE

About the Series

Legatee of a vast empire, the Commonwealth still carries the imprint of its past. And in doing so it may be said to have a collective identity which, in a very varying degree, each of its members exhibits. This, we believe, can sustain a collective inquiry into the political history and institutions of countries which were once governed within the British Empire and we note signs of a revival of interest in this field. In recent years 'area studies' have been encouraged, but there is also a sense in which the Commonwealth is itself a region, bounded not by geography but history, and imperial history in particular. Seen thus the region cannot exclude areas into which empire overspilled as in the Sudan, or areas now outside the Commonwealth such as South Africa and Burma, or the unique case of Ireland. No account of the dilemmas which face the government of Canada or Nigeria or India —or indeed of the United Kingdom—which examines the present in relation to the past can be complete which omits some consideration of this 'imperial dimension'. Without in any sense trying to claim that there is a 'political culture' common to all Commonwealth countries it is certainly the case that some of the institutions, some part of the political life, and a certain element in the political beliefs of many Commonwealth leaders, can be said to derive from the import of institutions, practices and beliefs from Britain into its former colonies.

Nor is the Commonwealth merely a useful category of study. It is also a community of scholars, many of them teaching and writing within the growing number of universities throughout the member countries who share an interest in the consequences of imperial experience and have common traditions of study.

The present series of books is intended to express that interest and those traditions. They are presented not as a guide to the Commonwealth as a corporate entity, but as studies either in the politics and recent history of its member states or of themes which are of common interest to several of the countries concerned. Within the Commonwealth there is a great variety—of geographical setting, of cultural context, of economic development and social life; they provide the challenge to comparative study, while the elements of common experience make the task manageable. A cross-nation study of administration reforms or of legislative behaviour is both facilitated and given added meaning; so also is an examination of the external relations of one or more member states; even a single country study, say on Guyana, is bound to throw light on problems which are echoed in Sri Lanka and Jamaica. The series will bring together—and, we hope, stimulate—studies of those kinds carried out by both established and younger scholars. In doing so, it can make its distinctive contribution to an understanding of the changing contemporary world.

Few problems have been more persistently and prominently on the agenda of Commonwealth statesmen in recent years than those of Southern Africa. Within that region no territory has more clearly presented itself as a peculiarly Commonwealth anxiety than Rhodesia since UDI. The present volume in the series aims to illumine this problem, not so much by retelling the by now fairly familiar tale of the course of events from 'Fearless', 'Tiger' and Geneva negotiations through the Pearce Commission to Lusaka and Lancaster House, but by examining the different facets of the country as it strives to emerge as the independent black state of Zimbabwe. The challenge it faces, as well as its potential for the future, are viewed in terms of economic resources and political forces, both within the country and in relation to others in the region.

DENNIS AUSTIN
W. H. MORRIS-JONES

From Rhodesia to Zimbabwe

Behind and Beyond Lancaster House

Edited by

W. H. Morris-Jones

Director, Institute of Commonwealth Studies,
University of London

FRANK CASS

First published 1980 in Great Britain by
FRANK CASS AND COMPANY LIMITED
Gainsborough House, Gainsborough Road,
London, E11 1RS, England

and in the United States of America by
FRANK CASS AND COMPANY LIMITED
c/o Biblio Distribution Centre
81 Adams Drive, P.O. Box 327, Totowa, N.J. 07511

British Library Cataloguing in Publication Data

From Rhodesia to Zimbabwe.
  1. Rhodesia, Southern—Economics conditions—
    Addresses, essays, lectures
  2. Rhodesia, Southern—Politics and government
    —1979- —Addresses, essays, lectures
  I. Morris-Jones, Wyndraeth Humphreys
  330.9' 689' 104   HC517.R43   80–49998

ISBN 0-7146-3167-1

This group of studies first appeared in a Special Issue
on 'Zimbabwe: Behind and Beyond Lancaster House'
of *The Journal of Commonwealth and Comparative
Politics,* Vol. XVIII, No. 1, published by Frank Cass
and Company Limited

Printed in Great Britain by
The Bourne Press, Bournemouth

Contents

Contents

Editorial Note

The aim of this collection of articles is to furnish information and perspective on the main economic and political elements present in the making of Zimbabwe. Although the articles were prepared before the conclusion of the Lancaster House negotiations, they discuss matters which must be central to the future of this important newly independent state of Southern Africa.

The articles by Mr Riddell, Dr Stoneman, Dr Clarke, and Mr Hodder-Williams were first presented as the 1979–80 Noel Buxton Lectures on 'The Economic Future of Zimbabwe Rhodesia' delivered at the University of London during October and November 1979 under the joint auspices of the Institute of Commonwealth Studies and the Noel Buxton Trust. The generosity of the Trustees of the Noel Buxton Trust in financing the Lectures and the planning and administrative assistance of Dr Shula Marks and Ms Margaret Beard are gratefully acknowledged.

January 1980   W. H. M.-J.

The essays in this collection originally appeared as a special issue of the *Journal of Commonwealth & Comparative Politics* (March 1980) under the editorship of Professor Morris-Jones.

Editorial Note

Notes on Contributors

Roger Riddell is a staff member of the Catholic Institute for International Relations, and editor of the Institute's Series 'From Rhodesia to Zimbabwe'. He was co-author of the 1974 Poverty Datum Line study of Rhodesia, and author of *The Land Problem in Rhodesia* (1978).

Colin Stoneman—Lecturer in Chemistry, University of Hull. Also teaches in the Economics Department and has written extensively on the Rhodesian economy.

Duncan G. Clarke has been Lecturer in Economics at the University of Salisbury, 1970–74. He was an economist for the Rhodesian Justice and Peace Commission and for the World Employment project at the ILO. He now free-lances.

Richard Hodder-Williams is Lecturer in Politics at the University of Bristol.

James Barber is Professor of Politics at the Open University. He is currently participating in a project on Conflict in Southern Africa at the Royal Institute of International Affairs.

John Day is Lecturer in Politics at the University of Leicester.

A. R. Wilkinson was formerly a Research Associate of the International Institute for Strategic Studies. He is the author of *Insurgency in Rhodesia 1957–73* (Adelphi Papers, International Institute for Strategic Studies, 1973), and of other publications on the war in Rhodesia.

Zimbabwe's Land Problem: The Central Issue

by

Roger Riddell

Catholic Institute for International Relations, London

'The land scheme is political and it is designed to ensure stability at the time of independence. It seeks to do this by giving European farmers a sense of security so that they may be encouraged to stay and by removing the tension from the land problems by providing settlement for those [Africans] who are suffering most from pressure on their own lands, where many have no land or insufficient land... If this is not done, a very serious situation could arise in which Europeans would evacuate their farms and Africans walk in. As the economy is an agricultural one to which European farming provides not only the bulk of the exports and of the locally marketed crops... as well as of taxation, this could bring economic collapse in the country. It is therefore imperative to take all possible steps to prevent this and both to give assurances to European farms and a sense of security and also to settle next year or so as many persons as possible from the densely populated African areas'.[1]

These words do not refer to the Rhodesian land issue; they were written eighteen years ago by the Kenyan Government after the second Lancaster House conference prior to Kenyan independence. They illustrate, however, two important points for any discussion on the land issue in present-day Rhodesia. The first point is that, as in Kenya at the time of independence, the Rhodesian land issue is highly political, most especially at the time of constitutional talks when the nature of the transfer of power is at the centre of discussion. The second point is the fear of the vocal European farming community that, without worked out guarantees for their future security, a constitution that gives wide powers to change existing institutions and structures is likely to lead to a mass exodus and the strong possibility of total economic collapse.

Although the land question is a highly political issue, the present discussion will not be making political value judgements or drawing parallels between the process of decolonisation in Kenya and Rhodesia. It is concerned with the economics of land today and the implications of past and present land policies for the economic future of Zimbabwe. This article is, however, entitled 'Land: the central issue' because it will be argued that the economics of land in Rhodesia and the fundamental economic problems arising from the historical division of land provide the key to understanding the main controversies over the future of Zimbabwe—political as well as economic.

In Rhodesia, as in nearly every other African country, land is important because a large majority of the population are directly dependent upon the land for their livelihood. Before the present war led to large movements of the rural population both across the borders to neighbouring countries and to the urban areas of the country, over 80 per cent of Rhodesia's population of seven million lived in the rural areas, the vast majority working directly in agriculture.

In present-day Rhodesia, land is of added importance for four inter-related reasons. First, access to agricultural land is extremely unequal: a small number of companies and individual farms own and/or farm vast acreages of land, while the vast majority farm very small plots. Second, there is acute land scarcity and growing landlessness in some areas alongside unused and underutilised land in others. This highlights even more the inequalities in access to the land. Third, the commercial agricultural sector plays a major part in the economic prosperity of the modern economy both directly and indirectly. Directly, it is the major employer of labour, the prime earner of foreign exchange, and the major supplier of internal food requirements. Indirectly, the commercial agricultural sector provides inputs to other leading sectors of the modern economy, particularly the manu-facturing sector, so making a further contribution to employment generation and foreign exchange earnings. Finally, all these factors receive added attention because of the way that racial divisions operate in the country. Landlessness, land scarcity, and overpopulation directly affect the majority of the rural African population who remain poor while the European rural population is the major contributor to commercial agricultural production and is rich in comparison. These four aspects of the land problem will be better understood if I elaborate the present situation of land, population distribution, and agricultural production in some detail.

The total land area of Rhodesia is 39 million hectares of which 33 million hectares (85 per cent) have been set aside for agriculture. Most of the remaining land is reserved for wildlife and national parks. Under current Rhodesian law, and also under the recently announced British constitutional proposals, agricultural land is divided into two categories, commercial land and Tribal Trust Land. Commercial land is open to purchase under freehold title, Tribal Trust Land is held under communal tenure by various tribal land authorities who are empowered to allocate arable plots to Africans in their jurisdiction and allow them access to communal grazing land, under the guidance of the overseeing Tribal Trust Land Board.

Before the passing of the 1977 Land Tenure Amendment Act and the 1979 Land Tenure Repeal Act, commercial land was divided racially into European farming land and African Purchase Land, 90 per cent being reserved for European freehold purchase or purchase by foreign or local companies and the other 10 per cent for African freehold purchase. As the recent legal changes have made little practical difference to the racial ownership and occupation of agricultural land, I shall continue to refer to the still commonly used pre-1977 categories.

The inequalities of land distribution in Rhodesia are apparent from the following. One hundred and sixty-five Tribal Trust Lands, which contain the vast majority of African farming units, cover 16.3 million hectares and currently hold about 675,000 farming units, giving an average of 24 hectares per unit. The European farming land consists of 15.2 million hectares and 6,682 farms, giving an average of 2,290 hectares per farm. Thus on average, each European farm is about 100 times as big as every TTL unit. In addition, about 2 per cent of African units are freehold farms located in the African Purchase Lands, each an average size of 185 hectares, less than 10 per cent of the size of the average European farm. These inequalities are reinforced by the differing qualities of the African and European land; the European areas consist of twice as much of the most fertile agricultural land as the African areas.

The importance of land in Rhodesia does not lie so much in the inequalities *per se*, but because inequalities in access to land are accompanied by growing overpopulation, landlessness, land deterioration, and increasing poverty in the African areas alongside serious underutilisation of land in the European areas.

Under the present system of mixed (arable and livestock) farming practised in the Tribal Trust Lands, the available productive land is able to carry a maximum of 275,000 farming units, providing a modest (i.e. low) income —given the present levels of capitalisation. Yet the Tribal Trust Lands in 1977 were carrying 675,000 units, two and a half times the safe number. In January 1979, the Rhodesian government published a rural development plan in which it admitted that the Tribal Trust Lands were holding 2.5 million people in excess of their safe carrying capacity: they should be carrying 1 million people but were carrying 3.6 million people. The majority of Tribal Trust Land cultivators farm plots too small to maintain their families; in 1976, average incomes from Tribal Trust Land farming were estimated to be about £12 a month for a family, well below poverty line income levels. In addition, there is a large and growing landless population; although no national figures of landlessness are available, the size of this problem is apparent from sample studies conducted five years ago in the south east of the country which showed that 40 per cent of rural men aged between 16 and 30 had no land. The extent of poverty in the Tribal Trust Lands is indicated by maize production and requirement figures. In 1977 the Tribal Trust Lands grew only some 60 per cent of their annual maize requirements and last year, with a severe drought, total production is estimated to have been 40 per cent lower than the previous year. The overpopulation and overuse of the land exacerbates these problems: over 17 times too much land is currently being used for arable cultivation; this land has been taken from the grazing land, half of which is either completely bare or heavily over-grazed. Each year, the land is becoming less and less productive.

Not all African farmers, however, are living in conditions of sub-subsistence. There are some comparatively large holdings within the Tribal Trust Lands which produce crops for the market and about half of the 8,100 African Purchase Land farmers could be classified as small-scale commercial farmers who market a large proportion of their produce.

In marked contrast to the overwhelmingly subsistence production of the overcrowded Tribal Trust Lands, the 1976 total of 6,682 farms on European land provide the backbone of Rhodesia's commercial agricultural sector and make an essential contribution to the growth of the modern economy. In 1978 total agricultural production was valued at £380 million.[2] Of this 80 per cent came from the European sub-sector which was responsible for over 90 per cent of total marketed output. Commercial agriculture contributes 19 per cent to gross domestic product, second only to the manufacturing sector, and it employs about 40 per cent of all employees, more than twice as many as any other sector in the economy. Rhodesia is self-sufficient in basic food production, with over 70 per cent of its national requirements originating in the European sub-sector. The main outlet for agricultural produce, however, is the export market, the main exports being maize, sugar, tobacco, and beef as well as smaller amounts of cotton, coffee, tea, and citrus fruit. Agricultural exports account for 37 per cent of Rhodesia's foreign exchange earnings, but as between a third and a half of raw materials used in the manufacturing industry originate in the commercial agricultural sector, agricultural primary and processed products earn about half of the country's foreign currency.

Agricultural production on European land originates from both individual European farmers and from companies, both local and foreign-owned. Large companies have almost total control over sugar, wheat, and commercial citrus production, with major interests in cattle ranching. Two companies between them, Lonhro and Liebigs, own over 2 million acres of ranching land. Individual farmers produce most of the tobacco, maize, beef, and cotton. In the 1977 season gross profits from European agriculture were valued at £164 million, 23 per cent of the total for the whole economy.

Impressive though these figures are, the overall contribution of European agriculture to the economy conceals marked sub-sectoral differences and considerable inefficiencies. Farms vary greatly in size both between areas of specialisation, such as cropping and ranching regions, and also within them. For example, in 1976 28 per cent of all European farms covered 77 per cent of all European farming land and were responsible for 79 per cent of total production; in other words over 4,000 of the 6,682 farms, covering 3.3 million hectares, contributed only 21 per cent of total European agricultural production. In that same year 60 per cent paid no income tax and 27 per cent of all farms contributed 95 per cent of all tax paid by the farming sector. Although over 4,500 European farms grow maize, in 1978 1,100 of them produced 60 per cent of the *national* maize crops.

What these figures point to is extreme variability in the productivity of European farming land. Some of the land lies completely unused. In 1976, before the escalation of the present war, at least 1.1 million hectares were not used at all. By mid-1978, the European farmers' union, the Rhodesian National Farmers' Union (now called the Commercial Farmers' Union) estimated that 2.8 million hectares of land lay empty. By April 1979 it was reported that 2,000 white farms had been abandoned and yet reports being received for the 1978–79 agricultural season stated that the drought rather than the abandonment of the land would be affecting production figures for the year. It seems that, with some 20 per cent of the European land area not in use, past production figures can be maintained.

As well as completely unused land, a considerable amount of land has always been underutilised. Using an extremely generous definition of underutilisation, the Rhodesian government recently estimated that 2.6 million hectares of land were underutilised.[3] If one assumed that by now at least 3 million hectares of land lies unused, then adding on the 2.8 million hectares of underutilised land would give us 5.8 million hectares, 40 per cent of the total European land area. Analyses of land use by agriculturalists and economists within the Ministry of Agriculture and the Agricultural Development Authority and from the University of Rhodesia, however, would suggest that nearer to 60 per cent of the European farming land is not being fully utilised.

One reason why considerably underutilised European farming land can still be farmed and why a proportion of farmers are able to remain on the land is because of the subsidies, both direct and indirect, which successive Rhodesian governments have given to the European farming sector. For many Europeans the original acquisition of the land has been due to loans, received especially from the Agricultural Finance Corporation, a statutory body. It is no secret that the white ownership of land is to a large extent conditional upon facilities from the Corporation. Since UDI long term loans to farmers have increased fivefold to the present level of £37 million. Some loans have not been repaid; for example in the four year period 1972–76 the exchequer reported losses of £17 million in respect of previous loans.

In addition to land purchases, the government has paid out considerable amounts of money for what it calls 'subsidies, losses and assistance' to commercial agriculture; in the five year period, 1974 to 1978, it paid out over £83 million. Some of this has been paid out to tobacco farmers in the post-UDI period in the hope of better prices in the future, some has been paid out in drought relief, and other payments have enabled inefficient farmers to remain on the land. More indirectly the Rhodesian National Farmers' Union has played an important role in assisting the government fix pre-planting prices for crops, and the relatively high prices have helped to keep the less efficient farmers on the land. While it is not being suggested that the farming community should not participate in fixing producer price levels or that the prices of inputs have not risen considerably over time, it does seem that the power of the farming lobby relative to other interest groups, such as consumers, has been considerable. To give one example: in April 1979, after initial consultation between the government and farmers, a pre-planting price for maize of $66 a tonne for the coming 1979–80 season was announced by the government. After objections by the Rhodesian National Farmers' Union, their asking price of $75 a tonne was agreed in August plus a generous bonus designed to increase crop acreages on otherwise unused land. With the Tribal Trust Lands becoming increasingly unable to feed their population, it is clear that one direct effect of this price rise is to place the burden directly on the poor consumer. A final indirect subsidy accruing to farmers relates to the extremely low wages paid to

African employees on European farms. For example, in 1977, over 80 per cent of the 240,000 African employees received cash wages of less than £16 a month; this is about half the minimum required for an average family.[4]

In spite of all these various subsidies, the Rhodesian National Farmers' Union admitted in mid-1978 that some 40 per cent of white farmers were technically insolvent. One is left with the conclusion that without considerable financial assistance, both direct and indirect, much more European farming land would be vacated or be seen to be seriously underutilised.

Thus far I have outlined the importance of land in present-day Rhodesia, and, implicitly, have suggested the need for land redistribution by pointing to the extreme overcrowding and growing landlessness in most African rural areas alongside substantial land underutilisation in the European rural area. But I wish to go further and argue that land is not just one important factor in the Rhodesian conflict but that it is the central issue, for it holds the key to understanding Rhodesia's economic structure and growth strategy. To do this it is necessary to broaden the discussion from the static analysis of the current rural land position to a more dynamic examination of why the present rural and urban structures have evolved and how land policies have affected major aspects of economic growth in the modern sectors of the economy.

The present distribution of land did not arise by accident, but by policies of successive governments who wished, with the critical help of foreign interests, to mould a particular pattern of economic development for the country. In the words of Robin Palmer, who has written the most comprehensive history of land in Rhodesia, 'Europeans . . . used their control over land to secure for themselves a position of economic and political dominance'.[5] From 1890 to 1923 Rhodesia was ruled by the British South Africa Company which initially hoped that to the north of the Limpopo might be found a second South African Rand. In the six year period to 1896 6.5 million hectares of land has been acquired by those eager to obtain mineral rights and a by group whom Palmer calls 'quasi-aristocrats, speculative companies, fortune-hunters and missionaries'.[6] The 1890s also saw the creation of the first African Reserves in Matabeleland. To the early 1900s, however, the European land scramble changed little in practice, largely because the Europeans at that time were not interested in using the land they had acquired and the African population continued to live on the land acquired by the Europeans. Indeed at this time African agriculture, particularly in Mashonaland, prospered as the Europeans were content to have African farmers provide them and their largely foreign labour force with food while they concentrated their efforts on mining. In stark contrast to the present situation, in 1903 European agriculture accounted for less than 10 per cent of total marketed output; over 90 per cent was supplied by African farmers.[7]

It was the next decades which saw substantial structural change in the colony's economic base as the British South Africa Company switched from mining to the promotion of European agriculture and both the Company and individual Europeans sought to control more of the land. To achieve this end two policies were necessary: one was to acquire more land and the other was to move those Africans from this land to the Reserves specially created for them. In relation to the first policy, by the time of the 1930 Land Apportionment Act, when the racial division of all land was institutionalised, 20 million hectares had been reserved for Europeans, of which only 30 per cent was being used at the time. In contrast the African Reserves totalled 8.7 million hectares under the 1930 Act to be increased to the present total of 16.3 million hectares during the 1950s and 1960s, although this doubling of land area for the Reserves is deceptive because the increased amount was largely unsuitable for dryland cultivation.

The second policy objective—moving Africans into the Reserves—proved to be a massive operation that continued up to the 1970s, the last publicised case being that of the Tangwena people in the Inyanga district. In the early 1900s only some 50 per cent of Africans were living in the Reserves and in Matabeleland the figure was nearer to 35 per cent. By 1910 the policy of African resettlement had begun, assisted by the imposition of a rent for those living on unalienated land. In 1923 the Chief Native Commissioner reported that the movement to the Reserves consisted of a continuous stream and by 1925 it was estimated that some 60,000 had been moved, nearly 10 per cent of the rural African population. Between 1931 and 1941 50,00 were moved, between 1945 and 1959 85,000 were moved, and since 1964 at least another 88,000 Africans have been resettled, the majority moving from European land, giving a total of 283,000 people.

Not surprisingly, the massive population inflow to the Reserves accompanied by the adoption of unfamiliar farming techniques and discriminatory policies against African agriculture led to an agricultural crisis in the Reserves. By the end of the 1930s, argues Palmer, the agricultural economy of the Shona and Ndebele . . . had been destroyed'.[8] As early as the 1920s, reports began to appear about the destruction of the land, over-stocking, and overpopulation, a story that has continued down to the present day.

The direct result of rural land policies has been to create a steady supply of Africans seeking work in the modern sectors of the economy which are controlled and owned by Europeans and local and foreign-based companies —on white farms, in mines, and in the urban areas—and to replace gradually the foreign African labour force which dominated both farming and mining employment in the early decades of the century.

The towns and cities of Rhodesia were always seen as European areas and, as early as 1906, 'native urban locations' were created adjacent to European settlements for the temporary occupation of Africans who were classified as migrants and who would have to return to their rural 'homes' at the end of their work contracts. The wages paid to this generally unskilled labour force were geared to the subsistence needs of individual migrants, no allowance being made for family members or for post-employment needs, while township facilities were rudimentary.

In the post-1940s period there has been a rapid expansion in urban employment, accompanied by a partial shift away from cheap migrant labour supplies towards the provision of a more stable labour force, particularly in relation to more skilled work. Average urban wages have risen and in 1960 the land laws were amended to allow a limited number of residential rights to Africans in their own townships. Even today, however, it is only a minority who are paid wages high enough to maintain their families in town and only a few thousand have incomes high enough to buy houses in the previously-white urban areas. In 1977 over 85 per cent of all African urban employees received cash wages below the austerely-calculated family poverty line and over 50 per cent received wages of less than half their minimum income requirements.

The European agricultural sector is the largest employer of African labour; in 1977 342,000 Africans were employed, nearly 40 per cent of all African employees. Here rates of remuneration are far lower than in the urban areas, even though more employees bring their families with them from the Tribal Trust Lands to live on the farm compounds. African employees in European agriculture receive on average only one third of the urban African wage. Most are totally dependent upon their employer for social welfare facilities and for food rations that go towards supplementing their low cash wages. In addition, many build their own houses and are allowed to cultivate small plots on the farms. Finally, wives and children take on temporary employment as seasonal demands require.

Through the creation of the African Reserves, the increasing inability of the Reserves to provide for the subsistence needs of a growing African population and the consequent steady stream of cheap African labour seeking work in the modern sectors of the economy, the structure of the present Rhodesian economy has evolved. And the expansion of the modern sectors of the economy has been dependent upon the continuing ability of the leading productive sectors—commercial agriculture, mining, and more recently manufacturing industry—to export their products. Using the indicators of economic growth and profits, this export-oriented economic strategy has been remarkably successful up to the mid-1970s, economic sanctions notwithstanding: gross domestic product tripled in the twenty-year period 1924 to 1943 and this was repeated in the period 1952 to 1972; the economy grew at over 5 per cent in real terms in the post-UDI period to 1975 and in this period gross profits rose from 37 per cent to 41 per cent of gross domestic product.

On the other hand, the present export-oriented growth path has consistently benefited a small European-dominated elite to both the relative and absolute deprivation of the African majority. While profit levels have averaged some 40 per cent of gross domestic product in the 1970s, only 27 per cent has been channelled to the African population, which makes up 96 per cent of Rhodesia's total population. Sixty per cent of the total population live in the Tribal Trust Lands and in 1977 the average monthly income per family here was £12. For those Africans working in the modern sectors of the economy average monthly wages were £40 a month.

In contrast, the average European household income was £535 a month. These differences are immense and in absolute terms have increased even in periods of high economic growth. Economic growth in Rhodesia is being achieved at the cost of widening wealth and income differentials and an increasing incidence of poverty for the majority of the African population. This suggests the need for change.

The need for change has become even more urgent in recent years because the modern sectors of the Rhodesian economy have become increasingly incapable of absorbing the growing number of African workseekers who are having to look for work outside the Tribal Trust Lands, so necessary because of the acute overpopulation and land deterioration there. In the period from 1966 to 1978 each year 175,000 African children either left school or were old enough to have done so had they completed their education. In the same period the number of new jobs in the modern sectors of the economy totalled 20,000 a year; and in the years of most rapid economic growth, 1969 to 1974, when the economy grew at 8.7 per cent a year in real terms, the number of new jobs totalled 33,000. Even when allowances are made for mortality, retirement, and those not looking for work it is clear that the Rhodesian economy as presently structured is just not able to provide anything like full African employment. The unemployment problem has not escaped the notice of the Rhodesian authorities. In 1970 the Treasury commented that: 'the imbalance of African children in relation to the size of the economy underlines the insuperable problem of creating sufficient employment opportunities in the money economy, however favourable external conditions become'.[9]

Drawing together the two main points from the above discussion leads to the following conclusions. First, an analysis of the present distribution of land and population and the relative use being made of the land points to the urgent need for a redistribution of the land. Second, Rhodesia's economy, as presently organised and built upon the land structure, is not capable of solving the critical problems of growing unemployment and widening income differentials, however favourable external conditions become. These points lead to a third conclusion: that if the development problems of an independent Zimbabwe are to be addressed comprehensively, then marginal changes in the distribution of land will not be sufficient. What is needed is a substantial restructuring of the land accompanied by a shift away from an externally-oriented growth path, dependent upon the composition of present exports which are dominated by primary commodities. Unless a more internally and self-reliant development path is taken, economic growth is likely, as at present, to be characterised by growing unemployment and widening income differentials.

To achieve these ends two basic conditions are necessary. The first is a government committed to achieve them and the second is a constitution for Zimbabwe which, in relation to the land issue, would allow a future government to embark on a programme of substantial restructuring. In relation to the first factor, one would need to move beyond the present discussion of economics to political economy and political analysis, for the choice of government is left to the votes of the electorate at a general election and the pressures placed upon people to vote for the respective parties. In relation to the second, I will conclude by examining some of the implications for land of the independence constitution for Zimbabwe tabled by Britain at the Lancaster House conference and agreed (with conditions) by both the Patriotic Front and the Salisbury administration. In offering these considerations, it should be stressed that the independence document published by Britain is not a legal constitutional document, but rather a fuller draft of the original proposals published at the start of the Lancaster House conference. It is thus not surprising that lawyers are not unanimous in their interpretation of the document.

In the proposed constitution opportunities for land acquisition in a future Zimbabwe are governed by the section 'Freedom from Deprivation of Property' under the Declaration of Rights. These rights are to be amended only by a unanimous vote in the House of Assembly and by not less than two-thirds of the members of the Senate for a period of ten years. The relevant part of the section reads as follows:

> Every person will be protected from having his property compulsorily acquired except when the acquisition is in the interest of . . . the development or utilisation of that . . . property in such a manner as to promote the public benefit or, in the case of under-utilised land, settlement of land for agricultural purposes. When property is wanted for one of these purposes, its acquisition will be lawful only on condition that the law provides for the prompt payment of adequate compensation and, where compensation is contested, that a court order be obtained. A person whose property is so acquired will be guaranteed the right of access to the high Court to determine the amount of compensation. . .
>
> Compensation will, within a reasonable time, be remittable to any country outside Zimbabwe, free from any deduction, tax or charge in respect of its remission. . .

The first point to note is the vagueness of the section. There is no definition of under-utilised land, though presumably it includes unused land as well, there is no precise definition of 'adequate compensation', 'prompt payment', or 'reasonable time to be remittable'. In addition, the section does not state who precisely is to decide whether land is needed for the promotion of the 'public benefit', although it is significant that it omits reference to the *government* deciding that the land is required for the public benefit, so suggesting that there be some 'objective' test of whether land be acquired for the benefit of the public. It appears that most of these problems of definition and interpretation are to be settled by the High Court, whose role in land resettlement becomes critical.

If we assume that the definition of underutilised land and the interpretation of 'public benefit' allow in theory for large areas of European land to be acquired (and there is controversy among lawyers on this point), then we need to consider the amounts of land involved and the cost to a future government of acquiring this land. As no indication is given of how land values are to be assessed, we shall assume that the High Court would use current land values as its benchmark for assessment of compensation.

The precise amount of European land which might be needed in a future land resettlement programme would be dependent upon various judgements: how many Tribal Trust Land farmers need to be resettled at once, how far a future government wishes to continue supporting a commercial agricultural sector oriented to exporting primary commodities, and how one defines underutilised land.

In a proposed scheme for land resettlement published by the previous Rhodesian government in January this year it was argued that 4 million hectares of underutilised land (26 per cent of European land) was available in the European area. The cost of acquiring this land at 1979 prices would be approximately £55 million. The plan proposes that in a ten-year period a maximum of 22,000 African farmers could be re-settled, the small number in part reflecting the poor quality of the land. This would be just over 3 per cent of the present number of African farming units. Clearly such a scheme would not solve the problems of overpopulation in the Tribal Trust Areas, nor would the extremely costly plans for developing certain Tribal Areas which accompanied the land resettlement proposals. Furthermore, the amount of land involved is considerably less than the 40 per cent currently available under extremely generous definitions of underutilised land.[10]

An independent study by the German Development Institute in West Berlin, published in November 1977, suggested that at least 75 per cent of European land would be needed to settle the excess population from the Tribal Trust lands, while at the same time maintaining a large-scale commercial agricultural sector for export and local production on the remaining European land. Clearly, more radical scenarios could be envisaged.

To calculate the cost of acquiring this 75 per cent of European land at current land values is far from easy for a number of reasons: land values vary considerably from area to area and are dependent upon soil quality, rainfall, and whether the land is suitable for crop or beef production; in addition within different areas land values vary considerably both in relation to the development of the land and to the extent of capitalisation—buildings, fencing, water supply, and irrigation facilities; finally many farms, even in the most productive regions, contain underutilised land alongside intensely cultivated land. To illustrate these problems, in 1979 European farms have been sold at prices varying from R$5 a hectare to R$486 a hectare. However, on the basis of a survey of European farms sold between June and August 1979 and excluding those sold for over R$200 a hectare on the assumption that this land would not be classified as underutilised—the total cost of acquiring 75 per cent of European land at current prices would be R$733 million or £480 million at present exchange rates. According to the terms of the proposed constitution, if this land were acquired, then compensation to present owners would have to be 'promptly paid' and be available in foreign exchange. The burden of this payment to an independent government would be far too great and would be in addition to other large foreign exchange commitments. As Rhodesia is at present desperately short of foreign exchange this money would have to be obtained in either loans or grants from abroad. Although Britain and the United States have offered financial help to an independent government, no specific amounts have been mentioned and recognising the enormous costs involved the British Foreign Secretary has argued that 'the costs would be . . . well beyond the capacity of any individual donor country'.[11]

To obtain large amounts of foreign exchange in order to finance the acquisition of European land would not only involve massive international assistance from bilateral and/or multilateral sources, it would also preempt other critically important uses of foreign currency needed for the huge reconstruction programme following the ending of hostilities and for other development schemes. In relation to land resettlement schemes, acquiring the land is only the first stage of the development process; the additional costs are unlikely to be less than 30 per cent of the acquisition costs, according to the small-scale plan worked out by the Rhodesian authorities. Within the present economic framework African farmers simply do not have the finance either to buy European farms or to put up 40 per cent of the purchase price as currently required by the Agricultural Finance Corporation in granting loans to prospective buyers. At the last count only twenty Africans had bought farms on previously European land in the eighteen-month period since the law had permitted them to do this and in May 1979 it was reported that over 90 per cent of registered African farmers were facing bankruptcy and some hundreds of African Purchase Land farms lay vacant.

Thus one is left with the conclusion that, even if a new government of Zimbabwe were committed to implementing a comprehensive land resettlement programme aimed at alleviating the acute pressures in the Tribal Trust Land, under the proposed constitution it would find it well nigh impossible to carry it out. In short, it appears that the proposed Zimbabwean constitution has been designed more to maintain the present structure of commercial agriculture than to address comprehensively the national problem of land. And this observation was made to the British Government by a former Rhodesian Prime Minister after the proposed constitution was announced:

> Land provisions should be designed to facilitate the distribution of land, not to frustrate both white land owners and black farmers who wish to co-operate. Your suggestions are not designed to meet the real needs of the country.[12]

NOTES

1. G. Wasserman, *Politics of Decolonisation: Kenyan Europeans and the Land Issue 1960–1965* (Cambridge, 1976), 130.
2. R$1 = £0.67 in October 1979.
3. In active cropping regions production levels of less than 2.1 bags per acre or 5.4 bags per hectare and in ranching areas an off-take of less than 30 livestock units per 1,000 hectares were considered to be underutilised.
4. An announcement by the Zimbabwe Rhodesia Government in November 1979 that the minimum cash wages paid to farm workers would rise to R$20 a month will not markedly alter this situation.
5. R. Palmer, *Land and Racial Discrimination in Rhodesia* (London, 1977), 1.
6. *Ibid.*, 35.
7. G. Arrighi, 'Labour Supplies in Historical Perspective', 6 *Journal of Development Studies* (1970), 209.
8. Palmer, *op. cit.*, 241.
9. E. W. Rogers, SJ, *Education for Socio-economic Reality in Zimbabwe* (Salisbury, School of Social Work Occasional Paper No 2, September 1978), 14.

10. In November 1979 the Muzorewa Government stated that in a future land reform
    programme the United African National Council (UANC) would make land available
    to 100,000 African farmers but no details of this scheme have been published.
11. Statement to the Lancaster House Conference, 11 October 1979.
12. Garfield Todd to Lord Carrington, 11 October 1979.

Zimbabwe's Prospects as an Industrial Power

by

Colin Stoneman

University of Hull

INTRODUCTION

Zimbabwe's prospects in general are clearly dependent to a considerable degree on the political outcome of the elections to be held under British supervision, and ensuing political realignments. In particular, policies affecting the relative priorities to be accorded the industrial and agricultural sectors, the private and state sectors, and the foreign and domestic capital sectors, will similarly be determined mainly by political considerations. So I shall make no attempt here to make systematic predictions or recommendations. I intend rather to list and briefly inspect a range of constraints and possibilities.

My main thesis is that the industrial sector is of comparable importance to the 'central issue' of agriculture. It has, however, been paid much less attention, and indeed has been almost totally ignored in the conference discussions. It seems possible that, although a fairly radical land re-distribution is the minimum to be expected in agriculture, the parallel issue of industrial redistribution may be forgotten or else treated to conventional solutions through lack of sufficient forethought. It is hoped that this paper will at least serve to initiate a debate. It falls into three main sections: (i) basic background facts; (ii) some relevant factors and their implications; (iii) the ownership of industry. (Throughout I use 'Rhodesia' to refer to the past and present regime, 'Zimbabwe' to refer to the future independent state.)

BASIC BACKGROUND FACTS

The diversity of resources

Rhodesia has often been quoted as being the second industrial power in black Africa, after South Africa. Although this may no longer be strictly true following Nigeria's dramatic oil-fuelled growth, it remains the case that the country's almost unique diversity of natural resources has led to a significantly more balanced and developed economy than any others in the region. Mining, manufacturing, and agriculture (commercial and subsistence) are all important—contrast the domination of mining in Zambia, Zaire, Mauretania, and some other countries, and the almost universal domination of agriculture elsewhere. But there is diversity also within sectors: in agriculture, tobacco, maize, sugar, citrus fruits, beef, and other crops and animal products are all important; while manufacturing industry has progressed well beyond merely the processing of local primary products, into both the capital goods industries and a range of import-substituting products; and in mining, six minerals, namely asbestos, gold, copper, chromium, nickel, and coal, are of comparable importance (with lithium, tin, tungsten, iron, phosphates, and limestone by no means insignificant, and platinum a good prospect). (Contrast the dominance, not just in mining but in the whole economy, of copper in Zambia, or of gold in South Africa.)

Some quantitative data by sector[1]

In 1975 (before a world recession and the war affected output seriously) the gross output of the agricultural sector was about £390m, and corresponded to a contribution to GDP of about 17 per cent; this may be compared with the 'under-developed' economies of Kenya, Senegal, Ivory Coast, Tanzania, and Malawi, where the contribution to GDP fell in the range 27-51 per cent, or the distorted economy of Zambia with 11-14 per cent over the period 1970-77. The gross output of the manufacturing sector in 1975 was worth about £1,000m, and the contribution to GDP was some 24 per cent (to be compared with 10-14 per cent in the other countries cited). In part this was because of the greater range of industry, but there are still some serious deficiencies, for example the lack of a petrochemical industry, and of any other than basic steel production or metal-working. The output of the mining sector in 1975 was worth about £170m, much less than the £500m from copper alone in Zambia (in 1973) or about £2,000m from gold alone in South Africa; nevertheless the industry contributed 7 per cent to GDP, much more than the less than 1 per cent for the other countries cited above except for Tanzania (1.8 per cent) and Zambia (36 per cent in 1970, falling to 13 per cent in 1977 because of the disastrous fall in the copper price).

The capital market

Rhodesia has the second most developed capital market in Africa after the Johannesburg Stock Exchange, so domestic resources are better mobilised than in most countries. Over sixty companies are quoted, including a number of major foreign-owned ones such as British American Tobacco, RTZ, Schweppes, and several Lonrho subsidiaries. Market capitalisation of quoted companies was almost $400m in late 1977. Gross Domestic Capital Formation was about 21 per cent of GDP in the early 1970s, not an exceptionally high figure, though better than many. It is claimed that only 13 per cent is from foreign sources (but see next section).

External orientation

The Rhodesian economy was of course originally a creation of foreign capital (the British South Africa Company) and designed to supply minerals and agricultural products (eventually tobacco in particular) to Britain and other countries. With the growth of the white settler population in the years after the Second World War (producing a highly urbanised community), import-substituting manufacturing and service activities began to reduce this, although the neglect of development of the black rural areas left most of the population outside the modern economy. Nevertheless, by the time of UDI, exports still accounted for some 47 per cent of GDP, with imports at 36 per cent. Clearly sanctions have helped further to reduce external orientation, but exports may still account for nearly 30 per cent and imports 20 per cent of GDP (the invisible balance more than cancelling the surplus). Almost all mining output is exported as is also a large proportion of tobacco, sugar, maize, and, until recently, beef. South Africa provides, and Zambia and other neighbouring countries used to provide, large markets for cheap textiles and shoes, processed foods, and simple electrical goods. Before UDI about half total investment came from externally owned sources. The claim that during 1971-75 only 13 per cent of investment represented new borrowing from abroad ignores the fact that some two-thirds of industrial investment is owned by foreigners, so that, although the resulting reinvestment (and for that matter, purchase of government securities as an alternative to keeping profits idle in blocked accounts) may have been generated locally, it nevertheless remains in the foreign sector and increases foreign liabilities. A truer figure for the foreign share in investment would thus be at least double that quoted, and possibly as much as 40 per cent.

The workforce

Total employment outside 'African agriculture' is about one million, of whom 12 per cent are whites. Of the roughly 900,000 blacks, over half are still employed on white farms or as domestic servants in white households, and thus have very low pay and no statutory minimum wage. About 60,000 (7 per cent) are employed in mining, and about twice this number in manufacturing. Formally recognised skills are very scarce among blacks because many avenues including apprenticeships were effectively closed until a few years ago. Whereas 100,000 whites work with some formal skill, it has been estimated[2] that only about 40-50,000 blacks can be considered skilled or semi-skilled. About half of these are teachers, there having been almost no other outlet for academically qualified blacks from O-level to postgraduate level until recently. There is as yet very little evidence of there being a significant number of formally skilled workers in manufacturing industry; in mining only a handful of the 1600 'A-grade' (skilled) workers are black, but there are

4,000 'B-grade' (or 'Advanced semi-skilled') workers, all of whom are black.[3] Although these men have been trained almost solely on the job, and are paid only about a quarter of the 'A's their job descriptions in the Mineworkers' Industrial Agreement are almost identical. Although no doubt less versatile, having had much narrower experience and little theoretical instruction, they would be unlikely to need much training should it become necessary to replace departing white miners. Although such direct evidence is not available in many other sectors, it would seem highly probable that a similar pattern prevails: even before the war began there was substantial anecdotal evidence (for instance quoted in reports and surveys) to the effect that 'unqualified' black assistants often worked adequately (and sometimes better) in skilled positions when their white (nominal) superior was away ill or on holiday. With the regular absence of a high proportion of white men on war service, there must be now very many more opportunities for blacks to gain experience in a wide range of responsible and skilled positions, and for longer periods, although without the results showing significantly in statistics.

Education

At independence Zimbabwe will probably have vastly more educated people than any other African country had (Zambia was said to have only a handful of graduates). Apart from some 25,000 teachers, there are many thousands of graduates in exile around the world or in the Patriotic Front forces (at least 6,000 and maybe 12,000 according to an estimate by the International University Exchange Fund), plus many thousands of present students. On the other hand it has been estimated that about half of all adults are functionally illiterate, and a similar proportion of the rising generation may grow up illiterate also. This is because even before the war over 25 per cent of children of primary school age had never been to school, and many of those who had had fallen out (largely for financial reasons) after a year or two. Now the war has resulted in the closing of a large number of schools.

The war

Disruption by war has had a profound effect right across the economy. Overall Gross National Income at 1965 prices has fallen from a peak of $1334m in 1974 to $1165m last year (13 per cent down), representing a per capita decline of 24 per cent from $220 to $165. In the mining industry exploration by major companies has ceased, and the volume index (1964 = 100) has fallen from almost 200 in 1976 to 172.8 in 1978. Similarly in manufacturing the volume index reached 208 in 1974, falling to 182 in 1977, although a slight recovery was claimed in 1978 and the first half of 1979. Most commentators agree that the war has had, and continues to have, far more profound economic effects than sanctions. Breaking of the latter by a British government would no doubt give the regime a psychological boost, but a continuation of the war would inexorably continue the attrition of the economy, and, probably, of white emigration.

SOME RELEVANT FACTORS AND THEIR IMPLICATIONS

The need for capital restocking

During the Federal period (1954-63) Southern Rhodesia received the bulk of the massive infrastructural investments that were made largely with public (state and foreign) funds. It is generally accepted that, rather unusually, the provision of such basic services ran ahead of demand from industry, so that Rhodesia entered the UDI period fattened up to withstand a long famine. Statistics of the efficiency of capital utilisation (output per unit capital) show increases up to the early 1970s. At that time the obsolescence of the railway system in particular became obvious, and major new investments were made in the rolling stock and track of Rhodesia Railways. Although some other large investments can be pointed to, for instance the notorious expansion of the Rhodesian Iron and Steel Corporation with European funds, the general picture now is of ageing and inefficient plant throughout most of private and public industry. The public sector investment programme published by the 'Transitional Government' required $3.5 billions at 1977 prices to be spent over the five year period 1980-84. One-third of this was earmarked for basic infrastructural development and a fifth for investment in the African agricultural sector (hitherto almost completely neglected). This plan requires investment in the public sector alone at almost twice the rate hitherto achieved for the whole economy, and the authors admit that more than half of this would have to come from foreign sources. This would seem to be quite unrealistic, given the existing debt burden, the needs of private industry, cost of various realignments of the economy (such as land redistribution), the lack of capacity of the building and construction sector to handle the planned projects, and other factors following in this section. It does, however, give a picture of the recognised needs of the economy following its 'milking' to maintain white spending power under sanctions.

Debt problems

The dimensions of the country's debt can only be guessed at, because declared public debt at $150m is smaller than in 1965, and almost certainly only a small part of the total in view of the rumours (indeed the necessity) for there having been substantial secret debts contracted, in particular to South Africa. There are also believed to have been loans raised on the Euromarket. Other short or medium-term debts include blocked funds owned by foreign capital, estimated to amount to at least $250m. In addition it is highly likely that rather than keeping all such funds idle, many foreign-owned companies have bought government securities on a large scale. Clearly the repudiation of some debts will be considered by a legal government, and such purchases, along with the secret foreign loans, must be among the leading candidates. The moral arguments for such a course will be reinforced by the severe burden on the balance of payments which would otherwise be incurred at a time when domestic investment will have to take priority. Long-term liabilities to private foreign companies and shareholders, a proportion of which may become an immediate payments burden once foreign control is regained, are estimated to amount to over £1,000m, and the annual cost of servicing this (interest, dividends, and profits) is even under present circumstances running at not much below $100m. (The last published figures for such payments were in 1974 when they amounted to $71m.)

Foreign domination of capital stock

Any recognised government, even one led by Bishop Muzorewa, will be obliged to take some action against the dominating position of the foreign-owned sector in productive investment. At the least this would take as a model recent South African measures requiring key companies to reduce their holdings in subsidiaries to 65 per cent or below 50 per cent in some cases. This will nominally be for reasons of economic nationalism, but in fact because neither the state nor a local capitalist class would otherwise be able to gain the authority to which it aspires. In addition the uncertainty of there being any net balance of payments gains from foreign capital (except possibly in the short-run only, if a new dimension of opportunities is in evidence) is being increasingly recognised. Current advice from economists in Rhodesia is to build on the significant holdings in companies quoted on the Rhodesian Stock Exchange by the various pension funds. If foreign companies were obliged to be quoted, with significant scope for local participation, then 'Pension Fund Socialism' could pave the way for domestic capital's relative growth. Later I will consider more radical attacks on foreign domination.

Other Factors

There is not sufficient space here to discuss all the other factors which will influence the prospects of industrial growth. Four, however, cannot be denied a mention. First and foremost is that even in a highly self-reliant strategy, Zimbabwe will remain a part of its region. Rhodesia's economy is highly integrated into that of Southern Africa: South Africa clearly, but Zambia and Botswana also, have been unable to sever many links despite a wish to make sanctions work. The principles discussed in this paper will need reworking in terms of the international consequences of any settlement: how rapidly dis-integration from South Africa can proceed; how closely to work with countries as politically different as Malawi, Botswana, Zambia, Tanzania, and Mozambique. Trade, transport, and industrial concentration will be the key issues on which regional agreement will be necessary. Second is the country's vulnerability to attack from South Africa in the event of what the latter sees as too radical policies, including expropriation of the assets of South African companies. Third is the near certainty that Zimbabwe will become a new 'Front-Line' state in the continent's confrontation with South Africa; apart from the possible consequences just mentioned, there is the point that foreign investors are likely to show a degree of reticence about taking up investment opportunities, however attractive a government chooses to make them. Finally we may return to the point made earlier concerning the diversity of the country's resources. This opens up a range of bargaining possibilities not available to one- or two-commodity economies, and with skill and forethought Zimbabwe should be able to drive a hard bargain with the foreign owners of its economy.

THE OWNERSHIP OF INDUSTRY

A key issue, but one that has been almost entirely neglected, is the question of the ownership of industry. Indeed one might, rather crudely, ask why the £1,000m agricultural question has received so much attention whilst the £1,400m industrial question is quite ignored. Or, rather schematically, is it that land redistribution may be consistent with the interests of a dominant capitalist class attacking a feudal remnant, whereas industrial redistribution is a socialist attack on capital? Whatever answers we may give to these questions, it seems clear that these two issues should be of comparable concern for nationalists seeking to build a reasonably independent state whose resources are used for the widest possible benefit of its people as a whole.

No-one can dispute that a situation in which some 6,000 rich farmers profit from the best half of the country whilst three or four millions subsist in poverty on the other half, must be ended. (It is not disputed by foreign capital, nor by the British government.) It would remain intolerable were the 6,000 black; but on the other hand the need for change is strengthened by the fact that the large majority of these people were supporters of UDI, that is, supporters of Rhodesia and opponents of Zimbabwe. But 'European' agriculture accounts for only around 11 per cent of GDP, while mining and manufacturing industry together account for about 31 per cent. If agriculture is the central issue for the here and now, industry is the key issue related to the major part of the economy and the potential for its transformation into an industrial power in the future. This industry is not merely also in the hands of a small rich white elite—it is to the extent of about two-thirds in the hands of foreigners. Only around a sixth of investment (mostly in infrastructure) is in state hands and will fall under direct Zimbabwean control. The rest is foreign or settler-owned. Whereas in theory many of the white farmers could become good Zimbabweans, helping to manage the farms they used to own, most of industry is not even owned by residents.

The foreign sector is therefore likely to wield power comparable to or greater than the state's in such crucial respects as investment policy, labour policy, the components of output, and influence on internal and external markets generally. Internal economic policy may in effect, as in other weak states, become merely a residual of world market conditions, mediated through the global calculations of companies whose

Zimbabwean operations are a small fraction of their total interests. There is therefore a crucial need, parallel to the need for agricultural resettlement, for a much greater involvement of black people in Zimbabwe's developing industry. In neither case is it sufficient that large numbers are *employed* (at low wages) by minority or foreign interests, and it would not be sufficient to replace a white elite by a black one. What is needed is a reduction in inequality from present levels which are among the most extreme in the world, and this implies a conscious government policy to promote state-owned industries, co-operatives, and self-managed enterprises, with a far-reaching reduction in the influence of external interests.

ATTITUDES TO FOREIGN CAPITAL

As stated earlier, even an unreformed Muzorewa government would be expected to move to reduce foreign ownership. There is common experience that foreign capital adapts quite happily, sometimes eagerly, to wider equity participation, state participation in joint ventures, even nationalisation (where marketing, management, technology, licensing, etc, remain under its own control). Loss of direct control during the UDI period will certainly have meant that there will be a backlog of rationalisation decisions to be made, capital to be realised etc. A conservative government, or even an unwary reforming government, could thus easily find itself heavily underwriting the costs of what might appear to be pro-nationalist reforms, but which would actually be strongly desired changes on the part of foreign capital, which would retain its domination of the economy at lower cost. Experience in many other newly-independent countries shows that foreign capital in general (though with the opposition of some companies) is only too happy to incorporate a section of the local population (entrepreneurs and state officials in particular) through devices ranging from the provision of favours and privileges through to blatant corruption; the population as a whole is generally little better off than under formal colonialism. The state has neither the will nor the power to control heavy outflows of income through such devices as transfer-pricing.

At a slightly more radical level, attempts to buy out key sectors could still leave the country economically dependent. This applies to the buying out of both white farmers and foreign industry. If, following the model of Kenya, a fund is established whose contributions are either provided locally or in the form of loans from Britain or the United States, then after paying compensation to the former owners, the state will be obliged to sell the assets to rich Zimbabweans (of whom there are far too few) or else loan money to poor Zimbabweans for the purpose. Three main consequences then arise: (i) the income distribution remains extremely unequal; (ii) the burden of debt and its servicing prevents the purchasers from investing adequately in improving (or even maintaining) the productivity of their farm or factory; and (iii) the purchasers become clients of the state just as the state is in effect a client of the rich countries sponsoring the fund. This is a recipe for inequality, stalled development, and economic and political dependency. The Patriotic Front have demanded in the case of land that compensation for expropriation should be Britain's responsibility, so as to avoid these consequences. But no assurances have been given on this. If such an outcome is unlikely for land, it may be taken to be impossible for industry.

The more radical the future government, the more hostile it will be to foreign capital. This hostility arises from at least three sources, apart from economic nationalism as such: (i) the recognition of the part that many foreign-owned firms played in sanctions-busting; (ii) the recognition that there are severe constraints on tackling effectively the central issue of rural development implicit in the existence of a dominant foreign-owned, market-oriented, urban-biased, industrial sector; and (iii) the knowledge of recent and far-reaching evidence that the costs of foreign capital go far beyond its expensiveness in balance of payments terms into structural effects which inhibit development and ultimately reduce even conventionally measured growth rates.

To illustrate this last point I will refer first to Albert O. Hirschman's 76th Princeton Essay in International Finance: [4]

> . . . the presence of a strong foreign element in the dynamically expanding sectors of the economy is likely to have a debilitating and corroding effect on the rationality of official economic policy-making for development. For, when newly arising investment opportunities are largely or predominantly seized upon by foreign firms, the national policy makers face in effect a dilemma: more development means at the same time less autonomy. In a situation in which many key points of the economy are occupied by foreigners while economic policy is made by nationals it is only too likely that these nationals will not excel in 'rational' policy-making for economic development; for a good portion of the fruits of such rationality would accrue to non-nationals and would strengthen their position (p. 7)
>
> . . . a considerable body of evidence suggests strongly that, after an initial period of development, the domestic supply of routinely imported factors of production is far more elastic than is ever suspected under business-as-usual conditions. If this is so, then the 'climate for foreign investment' ought to turn from attractive at an early stage of development to much less inviting in some middle stretch . . . (p. 6).

And secondly I draw attention to a recently published comprehensive review of sixteen independent studies of cross-national evidence of the effects of foreign investment on economic growth and inquality, conducted over the last ten years: [5]

> Our review of the evidence has produced the following assessment of the empirical relationships with which we are concerned:

(1) The effect of direct foreign investment and foreign aid has been to increase economic inequality within countries. This effect holds for income inequality, land inequality and sectoral income inequality. (2) Flows of direct foreign investment and foreign aid have had a short-term effect of increasing the relative rate of economic growth of countries. (3) Stocks of direct foreign investment and foreign aid have had the cumulative effect of decreasing the relative rate of economic growth of countries. This effect is small in the short run (1-5 years) and gets larger in the long run (5-20 years). (4) This relationship, however, has been conditional on the level of development of countries. Foreign investment and aid have had negative effects in both richer and poorer developing countries, but the effect is stronger in the richer than in the poorer countries. (5) These relationships hold independent of geographical area. (p. 677)

. . . foreign investment tends to produce uneven growth across economic sectors. Such uneven development may be one mechanism by which foreign investment leads to a lower rate of growth . . . foreign investment leads to increasing income inequality, early monopolization and structural underemployment, thus favouring early saturation of effective demand and lowering the rate of capital formation in a country. And since capital formation is a major cause of increasing growth, this reduction in capital formation is another mechanism by which foreign investment reduces growth. Finally . . . one of the ways in which foreign investment reduces growth is by reducing state power, and hence the ability of the state to undertake a policy of growth, independent of the class interests created by foreign capital. (p. 678).

SOME SCENARIOS

I will conclude by sketching in what seem to be the main possible outcomes in the industrial field. Of necessity these scenarios are brief, increasing the impression of naivety such an approach usually gives. Nevertheless if it is accepted that I am *not* implying that no other factors may enter, nor that no intermediate cases may arise, the exercise may serve to clarify the range of possibilities.

(i) Continuing foreign capital dominance. This would no doubt be accompanied by some mainly cosmetic concessions to nationalism, involving local equity participation, some joint ventures with government, and possibly nationalisation (with full compensation) in one or two cases. As Zimbabwe counts as one of the richer developing countries, the evidence referred to above, as well as theoretical considerations, would suggest that despite its excellent resources Zimbabwe's development would become stalled in the manner common in Latin America, with continuing poverty in rural areas and corruption in the cities.

(ii) An attempt to buy out foreign capital. In theory such a strategy could lead to self-reliant development. There is, however, no possibility of the necessary finance being made available from outside the country, and the only possible internal resources would have to come from the very sectors controlled by foreign capital. In other cases where it has been attempted to pay compensation from future profits, far too much room for manoeuvre has been left to the companies, so that either the enterprise has been run down in the transfer period, or inadequate provision has been made for efficient operation by locals. Given the likely total value of foreign capital—estimated at between £1,000m and £1,400m[6]—probably some two-thirds of total productive investment, the costs of such a strategy would probably severely constrain investment and thus future growth prospects in Zimbabwe. (See, however, (iv) below.)

(iii) Recognising the above consequences, together with moral considerations connected with sanctions-busting and past exploitation, the Patriotic Front has often tended to take expropriation for granted. This would probably attract two sets of consequences: (a) military invasion by South Africa, possibly covertly supported by Britain and the United States; (b) effective trade and technology sanctions from these powers. Such a strategy would therefore only be possible if underpinned by the type of guarantee made to Cuba by the USSR. It might then lead to independent development leading to Zimbabwe becoming a major industrial power in the area; much would, however, depend on the extent to which neighbouring countries cooperated in trade, transport, economic integration, etc, so as to prevent subservience to Russian interests.

(iv) The difficulties of the more radical options incline many observers to conclude that the only real option is to concede continuing foreign capital dominance, whilst seeking to reduce its disadvantages. There may however be a fourth option, drawing on some elements from the second and third, together with other ideas. One such (deriving originally from Dr Raul Prebisch of UNCTAD) is for a financial intermediary which could acquire foreign-owned assets holding them until placement can be made with local investors. But to quote Albert Hirschman again:

> One objection will surely be levied against the operation: Is it really desirable to transfer presently foreign-owned firms to local ownership when the new owners cannot but be drawn from the very small clique of already too powerfully entrenched local capitalists? History issues a warning here, for this very sort of thing happened in the second half of the 19th century when liberal parties came to power in a number of Latin American countries. The newly installed anti-clerical governments expropriated the sizable lands owned by the Catholic Church—and then proceeded to sell them at bargain prices to the landed elite. As a result, the concentration of landholdings became far more pronounced. . . . If foreign-owned

assets were to be sold directly to local investors, it would be impossible not to sell to the few and the powerful. But if an intermediary stands ready to hold the divested assets for some time, the outcome may be quite different. One attractive possibility is that the agency would sell, on the instalment plan, a substantial portion, and perhaps a majority, of the equity of the erstwhile foreign firms to white- and blue-collar workers, with first choice being given to those who are employed in such firms . . . . It is quite conceivable, moreover, that the foreign investors themselves would take a more benign view of divestment if they knew that their assets were to be transferred to their workers and employees rather than to local competitors or some public agency. (pp. 14-15)

One could go further, suggesting the establishment of cooperatives or self-managed enterprises. But the main other element required relates to both the time-scale of the proposed transfer and the principle on which compensation for divestment should be assessed. We may call the general strategy 'Planned Cooperative Divestment'. It would entail (a) a statement of the aim of attaining economic independence in five to ten years' time; (b) a requirement on foreign capital to maintain output, exports, and investment in the interim, *and* meanwhile to train local management and workers to take over at the end of a transfer period (which would vary for different industries and different firms, both for technical and for financial reasons); (c) an independent agency or agencies (possibly involving the United Nations) to assess the adequacy of achievement of these aims, so as to compute the appropriate compensation on a previously determined formula; (d) expropriation for certain firms guilty of sanctions-busting, those unwilling to cooperate or involved in sabotage (following the pattern in Mozambique), and as the ultimate penalty for those indulging in undercover expatriation of capital via transfer-pricing or similar detrimental practices during the transition period; (e) a general principle to maximise popular control of industry— for instance by requiring the present management to train (if necessary with advice from appropriate sources) the entire workforce rather than a substitute hierarchical management structure only. This latter point is important not just for democratic reasons, but also for technological ones. With the likelihood of considerable instability in the labour force, because of both the emigration of white workers, and the mobility of black workers as new positions become open to them for the first time, many individuals trained for a particular position may transfer to other positions with no trained substitute being available. In addition, in the early stages of black incorporation into the control positions of industry, many mistakes will be made, involving people who turn out to be unsuited to their initial choice of function. A high degree of flexibility is therefore desirable, coupled with a greatly reduced income distribution so that individuals do not have too great an incentive to hold on to prestigious positions for which they are unsuitable. Planning for workers' cooperatives or self-managed enterprises would appear to meet the requirements, relieving also pressures on government from the need to exert full state control. Lest it should be thought that this suggestion is unrealistic, it should be pointed out that one of the main characteristics of the present situation is of large numbers of educated Zimbabweans denied appropriate jobs for racial reasons (or else concentrated in the health and education services). Training in many cases could therefore take theoretical or background knowledge for granted, concentrating on control and technical or practical skills.

Although such a strategy would clearly benefit from outside finance, it need not be impossible in the absence of it. Few funds would be needed at the start, as initially there would be expropriation (without compensation) of non-cooperators etc. The first funds might be needed after about five years (the programme could be carefully phased) by which time following the ending of sanctions and war-time disruptions there could be greatly increased foreign exchange earnings from tobacco, sugar, and minerals in particular. Some of the more expensive compensations could be left until later, so that the base for funds could be augmented from earlier transfers to local control of profit flows. In addition, compensation need not be generous, both on moral grounds (many might argue that compensation is inappropriate in any case) and because the great diversity of the economy means that Zimbabwe could drive hard bargains with individual companies. Zambia, for instance, had little room for manoeuvre with the copper companies, for all knew that the country would sink without the copper industry. Zimbabwe would not collapse without its entire mining industry, let alone the one-sixth of it that is the copper industry, or without the cooperation of even the biggest firm in the industry.

CONCLUSION

No 'blueprint' for future Zimbabwean development is justified at the present stage of developments. It is hoped, nevertheless, that this paper has demonstrated that as well as there being a range of factors which could ruin Zimbabwe's development prospects (at any rate for the medium term) there would also seem to be present nearly all if not all the factors necessary for a viable self-reliant strategy. Given the political will to remain uncompromising on ultimate aims, along with skill in avoiding unnecessary provocation of powerful enemies, Zimbabwe could become a dynamic industrial democracy which would be a model throughout Africa and beyond.

NOTES

1. Data for the Rhodesian economy are taken from publications of the Central Statistical Office, Salisbury. Data for other countries from OECD, *Latest Information on National Accounts of Developing Countries,* Nos 7-10 (Paris,

1973-79). Estimates are taken from my earlier publications, in particular 'Foreign Capital and the Prospects for Zimbabwe', 4 *World Development* (1976), 25-58; see also Note 6.

2. C. F. Stoneman, *Skilled Labour and Future Needs* (No 4 in the series *From Rhodesia to Zimbabwe*) (London, 1978; Gwelo, 1978).

3. C. F. Stoneman, 'Skill Needs in the Mining Sector in Zimbabwe', in *Zimbabwe Manpower Study*, Report, Volume 3 (Geneva, 1979), 87-111.

4. A. O. Hirschmann, 'How to Divest in Latin America and Why', 76 *Essays in International Finance* (Princeton, 1969).

5. V. Bornschier, C. Chase-Dunn, and R. Rubinson, 'Cross-national evidence of the effects of foreign investment and aid on economic growth and inequality: a survey of findings and a reanalysis', 84 *American Journal of Sociology* (1978), 651-683.

6. C. F. Stoneman, 'Foreign Capital and the Reconstruction of Zimbabwe', *Review of African Political Economy*, No 11 (1978), 62-83.

Zimbabwe's International Economic Position and Aspects of Sanctions Removal

by

D. G. Clarke

I INTRODUCTION

This paper attempts to outline briefly two inter-related aspects concerning Zimbabwe's economic future. These are:

(i) the nature and changing character of the external sector especially in the 'sanctions period' (1966-79); and

(ii) the possible economic implications of sanctions removal.

Now, it is clear that this is a most difficult task to accomplish. Firstly not all the available evidence required for a proper evaluation yet exists on the public record, e.g. in respect of data on trade flows, investment links, and secret loan (and even aid) agreements struck over the past fourteen years. As a result, only an imperfect picture emerges—so leaving too much scope, and necessity, for hypothesis and imputation as well as statistical error. At the very worst, calculated distortion could even arise from unconscious or wilful dependence on ideological suppositions.

Secondly and perhaps paradoxically, although it partly stems from the first point, international economic aspects have not been the prime focus of scholarly studies on the economy. To some extent the neglect has been partially redressed in the last couple of years.[1] But it is by no means evident that an adequate story has been told.

Then there are other limitations relating to the character of this review which should also be acknowledged. It is brief, if not perfunctory on many important points, since time and opportunity have not permitted the sort of in-depth examination which the subject deserves. Moreover, there is a strong economic bias in the approach used; and hence political considerations, arguably of some importance, may have been under-stressed. All that is familiar *apologia* for economists.

Having made these caveats, it should also be remembered that Zimbabwe's position and recent economic experience have been fairly unique among developing countries and do not lend themselves, except in facile ways, to simple comparative analysis. It was only just over four

decades before UDI in 1965 that the country was still under the formal
legal aegis of a Company government, in this case the British South
Africa Company, formed under Royal Charter and funded with British
and South African venture capital. The high level of external economic
dependence which developed, as well as the contemporary presence of
many sizeable transnational corporations in the economy, owe much to
the institutional and structural developments flowing from this formative
period. More pertinently, no other developing country has been as subject to the wide range and duration of economic sanctions which have
applied in the Zimbabwean case. And yet, despite this, the economy's
growth record (apart from the last four years) places it in the category
of 'successful performers' in the third world. Indeed, it is this economic
growth pattern which forms the starting point of the present inquiry
and provides the background within which the issues of sanctions and
the external sector need to be situated.

II THE ECONOMIC BACKGROUND, 1966-1979

Despite recessionary conditions after 1959, the Southern Rhodesian
economy was still recording a positive growth rate in GDP and *per capita*
income in the years leading up to 1965. On the other hand, overall investment rates had fallen, African unemployment was growing and
subsistence sector production continued to move erratically around a
very low base level, mostly in accordance with seasonal conditions. UDI
was declared in these conditions of moderate modern sector growth and
increasingly visible structural problems of urban African poverty and
rural household marginalisation.

Sanctions and counter-sanctions

International policy initiatives taken against the economy, first by Britain
and eventually on a more comprehensive basis under Chapter 7 of the
UN Security Council enforcing a mandatory embargo, were in retrospect
at least one step behind contingency initiatives of the Salisbury régime.[2]
The shifting of sterling reserves from London and some oil supply
stocking in Rhodesia are two examples of those preemptory moves. The
'British theory' as it might be labelled, of sanctions precipitating massive
economic regression in 'weeks rather than months (or at least within one
year)' was soon put to the test. This test it failed. The underlying theses
of the model rested upon the evident vulnerability of the country expressed in its high import and export ratio to GDP, its lack of domestic
oil sources, a commodity-specificity and concentration in exports, and
expected internal 'multiplier effects' presumed to follow from reduced
external demand. Historical dependence on foreign capital inflows, imported technology, and expatriate managerial inputs through transnationals were also believed to be favourably arrayed towards the same
end.
    A broad range of economic constraints were applied. An organised,

UN-supervised trade and financial boycott ensued even though mandatory controls did not apply to all commodities and services which linked the economy to the outside world. On the import side, it was hoped that import dependent industries would soon close (for lack of spares and intermediate goods), so causing income and employment losses. On the export side, markets were targeted to become quickly and severely restricted and thereby foreign currency earnings and reserves perilously reduced. This 'scissors effect' was designed to precipitate a balance of payments crisis, cut real GDP, and ultimately force 'sensible' re-alignment in the political sphere. Sanctions were conceived and executed *as if* they would bite quickly and deeply. They did not or, at least, they were not sharp enough.

The apparent failure of sanctions *under this model* (it will be argued later that other serious effects ensued, for largely unanticipated reasons), might be ascribed to a number of factors.

First, as mentioned, preemptive moves were successfully implemented. This permitted a critical short-term breathing space which, despite important immediate sanctions effects, allowed time for longer term planning and comprehensive and defensive economic re-adjustments. It should be remembered, too, that local firms knew of the imminence of sanctions. Advance stocking and 'export-pipeline clearing' could thus take place on the basis of knowledge about more difficult trading conditions to come. The regime itself had already applied import control measures; and the timing of the announcement in November allowed the 'first round effects' to take place after the heavy throughput of seasonally-affected exports (e.g. maize and tobacco). A high 1965 growth rate and a visible trade surplus also reinforced the balance of payments position.

Second, the range of potential defensive adjustments eventually applied must have been underestimated in kind, degree, and impact. And these measures had increasingly offsetting effects as time went by and positive GDP growth ensued over the first nine years. A few notable moves deserve to be mentioned. For instance, on the import side controls were made more comprehensive and restrictive through the licencing of allocations, the cutting back on non-essential items, and the direct rationing of strategic commodities (e.g. oil and foreign exchange). These measures were complemented by a powerful import substitution drive, notably in manufacturing sectors. The establishment of new 'infant industries' behind the protective sanctions wall was also actively promoted—600-odd being inaugurated in the first three years. The domestic technical and managerial capacity for such adaptation, either ignored in the British theory or under-estimated, was fully exploited. Likewise, some excess capacity in export industries was diverted to meet new local needs. The accompanying shift towards direct state participation and increased central regulation did not itself in the end damage the economy. And the economy had the good fortune to have in hand excess infrastructural capacity from investments in the Federal period. In export spheres new markets were quickly, if not easily, found—with and through South Africa, some North Atlantic economies, and even in Africa.[3] Former traditional trade partners also took time to run down their commercial interests; and it is now also known that on some strategic items 'business as usual' prevailed, *albeit* in more circumspect form.[4] Third party transactions—via South Africa, (Portuguese) Mozambique, and elsewhere—made all this easier, if expensive. Changing export composition was also facilitated and was related to forced diversification in agriculture, notably against export crops (particularly tobacco). On the international financial front, 'it took two to tango'. Asset freezing was a two-sided affair which allowed the regime a net saving on the payments flow to Britain, Sterling Area countries, and international institutions. The short-term saving involved was not insubstantial.

Third, in terms of domestic economic policy, a series of manoeuvres shifted the sanctions impact away from high-income groups—through fiscal changes, direct subsidies, a move towards indirect taxation, and state support for affected enterprises and potentially unemployed persons with 'shiftable skills'. Local skills shortages in manufacturing, coupled with a proximate and easibly accessible as well as protected South African labour market, ensured a low level of actual white unemployment. To the extent that sanctions bit quickly and deeply, the thrusts were deflected from the political target group.

Fourth, two adjacent economies allowed for increasing *regional* economic integration in contradiction to the world-wide trend. This had major implications for trade, services, transport facilities, insurance, investment, loans, and credit arrangements. It also affected transnational corporate operations which continued, sometimes on a more rational basis, through South African-based subsidiaries of British, American, and Canadian companies. Nor did South African firms feel the constraints of international sanctions policy despite the Pretoria Government's withholding of *de jure* recognition. It was the *de facto* position which counted at the end of the day.

Finally, internal business opposition to sanctions—expressed for example by ARNI, the Chamber of Mines, the Institute of Directors, and others—quickly wilted under pragmatic necessities, compliance requirements under new legislation, and potential or implied threats from the administration. There is also the extremely important fact to be considered that trade and financial boycotts were not accompanied by *actual* disinvestment. So the show went on. Profits earned by foreign firms were re-invested locally under a new policy regime—so sustaining local market expansion and domestic employment levels. This component has formed a major share of gross fixed investment throughout 1966-79. (If nothing else, there may be an important lesson in this experience for the current debate about sanctions on South Africa.)

Enough then of certain weaknesses in the official sanctions scenarios of proponents as conceived and applied at the time. What of unofficial observations? Did anyone foresee the eventual course of events? To this question it can be said that at least two sources *ex ante* identified some important economic trends which would, and ultimately did, moderate or alter the impact of sanctions.[5]

For example, as early as 1967 a cogent and convincing demonstration (by Curtin and Murray) suggested that import substitution strategies would drastically weaken the expected effects of (then voluntary) sanctions application. It was precisely this aspect of counter-sanctions policy which was pursued with a vengeance over the short-term. The study also concluded that 'time [was] the most valuable commodity the Smith regime [had] at its disposal.'[6] Looking back this, too, seems to have been broadly correct for the medium-term, although as Keynes might have remarked 'in the long-run even Mr Smith will be dead.'[7] In fact it is precisely in this long-run period, the tenth to fifteenth year aftermath of sanctions declaration, that some important economic chickens have come home to roost. So it might be suggested that short- and long-run (as well as trade and other) effects need to be distinguished. (In a later section attention will be drawn to some of the *cumulative* implications occasioned through investment flow diminution and structural unemployment effects connected to the sanctions experience.)

It is worth noting too, that another perspective on sanctions (*circa* 1968), based on a cost/benefit approach, also gave the benefit of the doubt concerning survival to the regime.[8] Again import substitution strategy, trade evasion, and savings from mutual asset freezing accounted in large part for the conclusions drawn. On the other hand, the study raised optimism about the prospects of import substitutive industrialisation as a means to deal with the 'Achilles Heel' of structural unemployment. For these reasons, it concluded (not so prophetically) that 'sanctions against Rhodesia cannot work.'[9]

A series of intriguing questions therefore arises. First, could sanctions have worked in the short-term? Well, it is known that they did not do so in the Harold Wilson 'weeks rather than months' sense. So the answer is probably no. Was the failure largely linked to the success of import substitution strategies? This would seem very likely as the medium-term is considered although many other policy aspects were important underpinnings of the ten-year post-UDI growth which the record shows. In which case, were there also other key determinants (perhaps, say, upper limits to import substitution) to be taken into account? And were the principal effects of sanctions, unbeknown to the architects at the time, really only able to take on a long-run character, working maybe through mechanisms other than simple trade and income transmission effects? What really changed in the 1974-79 period? To this last group of questions most observers cite the escalating war and its direct and indirect costs on the economy in the form of asset losses, reduced incomes, unemployment effects, the diversion of monies to non-productive military outlays, skills re-allocation, and so on. Undoubtedly there are important points in these arguments. Yet is it a wholly convincing case? The key productive assets remain intact, income and employment effects may be more to do with recession, and skills are also more shiftable under recession. The only real strong point is the one affecting state investment patterns. To have a fuller picture, then, the performance of the actual economy and changing regional economic conditions need to be reviewed. In doing so one is less inclined to over-emphasise the singular war-effects dimension.

General economic trends

Consider now Table I which provides evidence on key macro-variables for 1966-78 (1979 figures are not yet available). The first year, 1965-66, saw GDP fall 2.6 per cent—a fairly *tiny* negative effect given the high growth of 1965 alongside the relatively traumatic conditions of the ensuing year. As the table illustrates, GDP (constant 1965 prices) grew systematically thereafter, reaching an all time peak of $1,354 million (81 per cent above 1966 levels) in 1974. The small dip of 1966 is to be seen as fairly unimportant in the changes over 1963-66, a period in which output rose positively in real terms. One is left to conclude that the expected short-term growth diminution postulated in the orthodox trade-income transmission model of sanctions was a much over-rated phenomenon in practice. This impression is reinforced when the actual size of the terms of trade effects of 1965-66 are observed (an 18.2 point fall in barter terms of trade, a massive estimated 45 per cent fall in the *income* terms of trade).[10]

But economic decline did eventually transpire after 1974. Yet this was surely closely in line with international and regional trends. In the first instance the country was no exception to OPEC oil price rises in 1973. As an industrialising developing country under oil sanctions, it was in fact 'doubly exposed'. Less directly the economy was much influenced by the world recession following OPEC's first substantial price adjustments. The illegal trading partners of the sanctioned economy experiencing these effects in due course passed them down the line in terms of higher oil *and* non-oil product prices. But this in itself is not the full story. South Africa was even more seriously affected by the recession than most. Its trading exposure and industrialised needs then far exceeded Rhodesia's. Finally, events coincided with the effects of the 1973 Zambian border closure as well as events leading up to and the onset of Mozambican independence in 1975. The Mozambique border closure, later in the day, added to the squeeze and allowed for more effective sanctions enforcement. Landlocked, under seige, and in the throes of an escalating war, the country found itself isolated from important outlets and totally dependent on the grace of a long-standing partner itself under severe economic duress.

Growth and decline in average living standards are also shown in *per capita* trends, these reflecting overall GDP trends with one important qualification (shown in the annual *movement* of growth rates). This was that in the period of growth, *per capita* expansion consistently fell under the rate for overall GDP growth; and, conversely, in the period of decline the same tendency applied. The results were traumatic. In 1978 real GDP stood at a level approximate to 1972; and GDP per head was akin to 1967. Today the latter index may well be inferior to the pre-

TABLE I: Zimbabwe: Changes in Macro-economic Indicators, 1966–78

	(1) Gross Domestic Product				(2) Wage Employment (thousands)			(3) Annual Changes in Total Employment		(4) Corporate Gross Operating Profits	
	Total (1965 prices)	Per Capita (1965 prices)	Real Growth Rates (Constant 1965 prices) Total	%	African	Non-African	Total	Number	%	Total	% GNI[a]
1966	749.5	161.9	1.7	−1.3	644	91	735	−13	−1.74	130.2	18.2
1967	810.0	169.1	8.1	4.4	659	92	751	+16	+2.18	158.0	19.9
1968	825.8	166.5	1.9	−1.5	693	97	790	+39	+5.19	173.0	20.8
1969	945.3	184.3	15.1	10.7	735	100	835	+45	+5.69	216.4	21.9
1970	984.0	185.3	4.1	0.5	750	104	854	+19	+2.27	252.0	23.8
1971	1,098.3	199.7	11.6	7.8	783	109	892	+38	+4.49	298.9	23.9
1972	1,201.1	211.1	0.3	5.7	840	113	953	+62	+6.95	365.6	26.6
1973	1,244.3	211.3	3.6	0.0	882	116	998	+45	+4.72	444.9	29.4
1974	1,359.1	223.6	1.2	5.8	923	118	1,041	+43	+4.31	560.1	30.7
1975	1,339.1	213.0	−1.5	−4.7	934	121	1,055	+14	+1.34	561.9	28.5
1976	1,318.5	202.8	−1.6	−4.7	919	120	1,039	−16	−1.51	569.9	26.9
1977	1,227.0	182.9	−7.0	−9.8	901	117	1,018	−21	−2.02	532.5	24.5
1978	1,182.8	168.0	−3.6	−8.1	n/a	n/a	991	−27	−2.65	534.0	23.6
1979 (latest)	n/a	n/a	n/a	n/a	n/a	n/a	n/a	n/a	n/a	n/a	n/a

TABLE I: Zimbabwe: Changes in Macro-economic Indicators, 1966–78—(cont'd).

| | (5) | (6) | (7) Annual Changes Consumer Prices | | | (8) Stock Exchange Indices (1964=100) | | (9) Terms of Trade^c | |
	Rate of Growth GFCF^b	Implicit GNP Deflator	Low Income All Items	Food	High Income All Items	Value of Turnover	Industrial Share Prices	Net Barter (1964=100)	Income T o T (1965=100)
1966	−13.8	3.1	3.1	4.0	2.6	38.6	129.8	82.3	54.9
1967	24.2	−4.4	1.6	1.9	2.0	40.9	154.2	79.8	53.4
1968	45.2	3.5	2.3	2.1	2.2	88.5	225.7	82.9	52.1
1969	−4.3	3.9	0.1	0.0	2.8	118.4	307.4	86.1	64.4
1970	20.3	3.4	2.1	2.0	3.5	85.4	268.9	85.6	70.3
1971	24.2	3.4	3.0	2.3	3.0	78.8	271.2	81.2	72.7
1972	15.7	4.7	2.8	2.8	4.4	110.7	344.9	82.4	88.1
1973	27.4	6.4	3.1	3.4	3.6	131.0	414.2	85.1	n/a
1974	27.1	10.1	6.6	7.0	7.5	174.4	460.1	81.9	n/a
1975	12.0	9.3	10.0	12.5	7.7	93.3	375.1	79.9	n/a
1976	−14.6	9.6	11.6	8.8	8.9	94.5	343.2	74.3	n/a
1977	−2.3	9.4	12.0	11.4	9.6	76.3	264.8	68.7	n/a
1978	n/a	8.7	9.8	10.0	6.6	102.1	285.2	62.8	n/a
1979	n/a	n/a	15.4	16.2	14.1	220.0	286.0	n/a	n/a
(latest)			(Jan–June)	(Jan–June)	(Jan–June)				

Sources: CSO, Monthly Digest of Statistics (Salisbury, various); also CSO National Accounts and Balance of Payments of Rhodesia 1977 (Salisbury, 1978)

Notes:
a. GNI refers to Gross National Income.
b. GFCF refers to Gross Fixed Capital Formation.
c. Net Barter Terms of Trade refer to the value index of exports divided by the unit value of imports. The Income Terms of Trade refer to the value index of exports divided by the unit value of imports. The latter are re-calculated on a 1965 base from R. J. Davies, 'Rhodesia's Terms of Trade', 8 Rhodesian Journal of Economics (September, 1974). No calculations are available after 1972 since the CSO has ceased publishing separate unit value series for exports and imports.

UDI period even though some easing of the negative trend emerged this year.

Now all this omits reference to various crucial distributive effects of wealth and income change brought about over the years. This is not the occasion to examine this facet in detail but consider briefly the movements in wage employment which can be used as a surrogate for some aspects of this issue. Column 2 of Table I illustrates the positive wage employment growth which accompanied output expansion—in all years up to 1975. It can be readily observed, however, that job expansion rates were always *under* those necessary to 'clear' annual inflows on to the labour market, let alone deal with the jobless backlog. Indeed, they began to wane as early as 1972 and became negative in 1975. Finally, the decline in the rate, and eventually in absolute numbers, related largely to African workers.

Corporate gross operating profits fared little better. They maintained an increasing share of a rising real GDP throughout 1966-74. The eventual slippage left 1978 levels no worse than in 1970 but nonetheless still much reduced in real valute terms. No longer either could the high rates of gross fixed capital formation, fuelled substantially by re-invested earnings, be sustained under these conditions. Real investment fell. Falling investment—coupled now with a sizeable diversion of state outlays to military activities and a generally rising inflation rate—brought about an economic recession having its most severe results among the unemployed, the rural poor, and lower-income employees in all sectors. In short, these latter-mentioned factors should perhaps caution analysts to examine quarters other than merely trade flow patterns for the very significant effects which sanctions had on the economy. Indeed, as will now be argued, the investment-profits-employment and poverty links have been the very spheres in which long-term sanctions impact has been determinant. These may have been effects *different* from the ones originally envisaged by sanctions applying countries. They may also have been of a *delayed* character. They most certainly were partly concealed by use of an eventually exhaustible set of internal policy manoeuvres. But they have arisen nonetheless; and for good reason they ought not to be ignored in the debate on sanctions impact. Before coming to this issue, however, consider the more detailed movements in the balance of payments over the period (Table II).

III THE EXTERNAL SECTOR UNDER SANCTIONS

The key features of Zimbabwe's post 1965 balance of payments can be readily summarised in aggregate. (Unfortunately, a restricted availability of data forecloses the possibility of a detailed item-by-item review.)

Balance of Payments Trends

The sharp almost 'once-off' 18 per cent fall in the terms of trade has

TABLE II: *Zimbabwe Balance of Payments: Current and Capital Account*
($ million)

	1966	1967	1968	1969	1970	1971	1972	1973	1974	1975	1976	1977	1978
Merchandise, net[a]	29.7	10.8	−22.0	32.0	27.9	3.1	62.1	88.9	59.5	31.9	155.2	132.8	178.1
Invisible transactions, net	−33.5	−27.0	−27.1	−27.4	−40.4	−58.5	−59.7	−103.9	−139.9	−160.5	−155.4	−157.2	−163.3
Services	−10.2	−13.5	−11.2	−5.3	−16.8	−24.8	−21.8	−58.5	−81.3	−92.8	−80.3	−96.7	−114.2
Investment income	−19.2	−13.4	−14.9	−17.8	−21.0	−30.4	−35.1	−38.5	−39.8	−41.2	−51.9	−45.2	−34.5
Transfers	−4.1	−0.1	−1.0	−4.3	−2.6	−3.3	−2.8	−6.9	−18.8	−26.5	−23.2	−15.3	−14.6
Net balance on current account	−3.8	−16.2	−49.1	4.6	−12.5	−55.4	2.4	−15.0	−80.4	−128.6	0.2	−24.9	14.8
Capital transactions, net	−4.6	23.7	39.5	9.9	26.3	30.5	−2.3	51.6	62.6	105.4	29.0	−22.2	16.6
Total current and capital transactions[b]	−8.4	7.5	−9.6	14.5	13.8	−24.9	0.1	36.6	−17.8	−23.2	28.8	47.1	31.4

a. Allowance made for non-monetary gold, internal freight to border, as well as timing and coverage adjustments in the computation of merchandise trade.

b. Balanced by short-term financing, changes in banking reserves, errors and omissions.

Source: CSO, *Monthly Digest of Statistics* (Salisbury, various): Ministry of Finance, *Economic Survey of Rhodesia, 1978* (Salisbury, April 1979).

already been mentioned. Another reversal, more graduated in nature but still important in terms of timing, followed the post-1974 international recession, causing a steady erosion in the terms of trade. In consequence, 1978 terms of trade were 26.3 per cent below 1973 levels and 37.2 per cent below 1964 levels.

Because of its isolation and the need to keep a close rein on international transactions, the regime in large measure subordinated domestic policy to balance of payments considerations. A (small) trade deficit only occurred in one year (1968). In the others, and increasingly in the 1970s, trade surpluses have been the order of the day. This has largely been a function of rigorous import control (with real import values in 1972, for instance, being kept *below* 1965 levels) and a strong export orientation stimulated through (partially subsidised) primary industries. While exact details on import/export volumes and values are not available since 1972, this structural pattern is likely to have continued to prevail. Re-exports have undoubtedly played a diminishing relative role in earnings as non-monetary gold transactions may have only become more significant since the 1971 Smithsonian Agreement and the establishment of a 'free' price for gold on world bullion markets. It is not known by exactly how much net internal freight costs might have increased but at least as of 1972 these were at manageable ratios (4.1 per cent) of exports and imports.[11]

What altered drastically was net payments for invisibles. These sums have mounted in each year since 1967 and the bill in 1978 stood five times higher (in current prices) than in 1966. Most of this price rise here dates to the early 1970s. A large portion probably relates to insurance costs and world oil and external transport charges. Some measure of the oil price effects is given by the fact that domestic retail petrol prices in mid-1979 were 336 per cent above 1973 levels and 51 per cent above those of a year ago.[12] Transit freight earnings, too, may well have dropped (as reflected in Rhodesia Railways deficits) except in the last few months in respect of Zairean/Zambian copper and import shipments.

Current account investment income outflows on a generally rising trend have also been a consistent feature of the last fifteen years. Some of this will have been on 'personal account', a component which will have risen with net emigration rates. But the bulk undoubtedly relates to corporate sector flows. On the other hand, these short-term movements have become relatively smaller in net effect as compared to total current account transactions in the last two or three years.

A more interesting aspect is the movements of investment income *and* net-capital transactions taken together. In this quarter UDI brought a sharp deterioration over 1966-68 and most of the adverse movements in income and assets engendered related to private companies. Only in 1970 did net capital transactions once again properly exceed the outflow of investment income although the cumulative level was temporarily above in 1968. It is thus important to acknowledge that foreign capital inflows have been significant in the stabilisation of the economy's balance of payments, in supporting the investment pattern, and ultimately in growth performance. Indeed, given the consistent current account deficit (in all but three years), capital flows have enabled a much more satisfactory record to be achieved on the balance of payments.

There appears, however, to have emerged a noticeable weakening of the balance of payments *structure* since 1974. In the five years 1974-78, deficits were run on three occasions, to an extent that a net deficit prevails for the period taken as a whole. In brief, this has largely meant reserve depletion at a time when foreign currency was scarce, growth was needed, and import allocations acted as a brake on expansion. The evidence on balance of payments trends, although incomplete, therefore tends to suggest that the effects of sanctions on trade flows, on induced price increases for services, on rising investment income and transfer outflows, and on the current account deficit have all become more serious over the longer-term. This has generated damaging consequences which sanctions theorists might have hoped for in the very short-run. Yet the fact remains that, as with the dampening of the manufacturing boom and the decline in GDP from 1974, these have only been longer-period phenomena. To illustrate this point more vigorously, consider now some connections between trade constraints and investment in the economy.

Sanctions-induced trade effects and investment consequences

It is now a widely used rule-of-thumb measure that the net discount effect of sanctions on gross trade flows currently amounts to about 15-20 per cent, i.e. because of import cost premiums and export discount losses the economy forfeited this proportion of revenue from trade.[13] The exact reliability of this measure has not been established, as far as is known. Until the country's trade data are de-classified, the issue will remain unclear. But as can be seen from Table I, the rule-of-thumb measure is lower than the 'first-order' terms of trade effect experienced in 1966; and, moreover, there have only been two years (1969-70) in which barter terms of trade were (marginally) above a level of 85 per cent of the 1965 index. In other words, use of a net 15 per cent discount on gross values seems at least a conservative order of magnitude measure of losses induced.

Two static, short-term, and ahistorical theses on sanctions impact

Strangely, however, in using this discount estimate most observers have also restricted their calculations to a single year. In particular, it is currently and widely applied as a means to estimate the sort of trade revenue *benefits* which might theoretically result from sanctions lifting in the *first year* of such a policy. Now with other arguments (examined shortly) the thesis has accordingly been developed in the conventional wisdom that sanctions-lifting will not confer substantial economic gains on Zimbabwe. The view is also often allied to subsidiary notions that sanctions in the past have not really worked or had much impact. Superficially there appears a consistency in these arguments which some would see as evidenced, furthermore, in the long-term survival of the regime and the failure of sanctions directly to induce short-term political change.

An opposing view, which might be called the *official wisdom* (of the regime itself), is that sanctions in the past have not proved a critical determinant.[14] Paradoxically, official wisdom has long held to this belief but it is now argued that it is only sanctions-removal which really matters. This body of thought has a short-run optimistic outlook, expressed crudely as 'lift sanctions, stand back for the "take-off", and watch ensuing development resolve current difficulties'.[15]

Now, all will be aware that important political theses underpin both these sets of arguments. But that does not make either empirically correct. The 'conventional wisdom' lobby is generally disinclined to see sanctions lifted even though paradoxically it is argued there will be zero result flowing from this change. The 'official wisdom' bloc for its part *now* foresees no other change other than sanctions removal as being of great consequence. Can these ideas be squared with evidence on the realities?

An alternative view: trade income losses qua foregone investment

Some of the confusion can perhaps be removed by a clearer impression of the *historical* record and by taking the long-term view of the past (and the future) to which reference has already been made. For it is not only the *size* of the annual (e.g. terms of trade) effect which matters but also the *compound* structural results deriving over time. Return now to the 15 per cent discount effect (one point on which *both* wisdoms tend to agree). However, consider this 'loss' on an annual basis over 1966-78 and think of it as an *investment capital* loss, i.e. if it had been earned, assume it could all have been invested with no absorptive capacity constraint. Some implications of this approach are spelt out in quantitative terms in Table III.

Firstly, it is noticed that the value of losses (column 2) rise in each year, from $41 million in 1966 to $103 million in 1978. This follows because of expanding trade values *despite* an acknowledged diminishing share of imports and exports to GDP (down from 51.5 per cent at the beginning of the period to an *estimated* 39.0 per cent in 1978).[16] The magnitude of potential investment loss can be compared as a share of actual *gross* fixed investment (column 5). The portion starts from a very high level, declines to 20.3 per cent in 1975 and picks up thereafter. In all years it is not inconsiderable. Here it must be pointed out that the investment loss is probably heavily *under-estimated* in a number of ways. Most importantly, the share would be far higher if the comparison were made, as it strictly ought to be, with actual *net* investment levels. Then one must remember that it is the lower end of the estimated discount rate (15 per cent as opposed to 20 per cent), which has been used. And, finally, it is possible to argue with conviction that the discount rate could have risen over time; so that in the late 1970s it might be measured above 20 per cent. But ignore these qualifications. They strengthen rather than weaken the case presented here.

Seen against net capital inflows (column 4), it is also apparent that the trade discount loss must have represented a major cost. Indeed, only in 1975 did the latter exceed the former. The relevance of this com-

TABLE III: *Long-term Sanctions 'Terms of Trade' Effects ($ million)*

	(1)	(2)	(3)	(4)	(5)	(6)
			Gross Fixed			
	$M+X$		Investment	Net		Theoretical
	(% GDP in	*15%*	*(% GDP in*	*Capital*	*(2)/(3)*	*inflow level*
	parentheses)[a]	*cost*[b]	*parentheses)*[c]	*Inflows*	*%*	*(2)+(4)*
1966	356.6 (51.5)	41.0	81.7 (11.8)	−4.6	50.1	36.4
1967	368.8 (49.6)	42.4	101.5 (13.6)	23.7	41.7	67.1
1968	382.9 (47.4)	44.0	147.4 (18.3)	39.5	29.8	83.5
1969	418.3 (44.2)	48.1	141.1 (14.9)	9.9	34.1	58.0
1970	488.3 (47.3)	56.2	169.8 (16.4)	26.3	33.1	82.5
1971	559.5 (47.3)	64.3	215.9 (18.3)	30.5	29.8	94.8
1972	602.6 (44.8)	69.3	249.9 (18.6)	−2.3	27.7	67.0
1973[d]	602.0 (44.0)	69.2	323.4 (21.5)	51.6	21.4	120.8
1974	762.8 (43.0)	87.7	411.6 (23.2)	62.6	21.3	150.3
1975	814.4 (42.0)	93.6	461.0 (23.8)	101.7	20.3	195.3
1976	853.6 (41.0)	98.1	393.8 (18.9)	25.7	24.8	123.8
1977	852.4 (40.0)	98.0	384.8 (18.1)	−22.2	25.4	75.8
1978[e]	895.8 (39.0)	103.0	390.5 (17.0)*	16.6	26.4	119.9

* estimate   M = imports   X = exports

Sources: CSO, *Monthly Digest of Statistics,* (Salisbury, various); CSO, *National Accounts and Balance of Payments of Rhodesia, 1977* (Salisbury, October 1978).

Notes:
a. Exports inclusive of re-exports.
b. Assumption of a *gross* discount on import and export values has been made.
c. Excludes re-investments in external companies.
d. No separate import and export data are published for 1973 onwards. Figures used here have been estimated at a *constant but declining fraction* of historical GDP (market prices). This may be a conservative proportion for 1975 onwards since GDP declined in real terms after that date.
e. The 1978 import and export values compare conservatively with the Standard Bank's estimates of $600 million for exports and $420 million for imports. See Standard Bank, *Economic Bulletin,* 19 September 1979.

parison deserves special attention since forfeited trade revenues in this case have a critical quality. If considered as a net investment loss, they imply also a direct foreign exchange liability. This flow therefore has all the financial characteristics of net foreign capital foregone, the *potential* implications of which can be read in column 6 which shows the 'theoretical inflow' that might have pertained if actual net capital inflows were added to the trade discount figure. If this had occurred it would have given both greater growth and stability to capital investment as well as more strength to the balance of payments. There is little need to spell out the GDP growth and employment implications of what has not happened.

If the arguments advanced here can be accepted (even with admissible qualification), it would seem to shed light on historical interpretations of the size and character of sanctions effects. It also provides evidence to evaluate the empirical bases to contemporary wisdoms about the real meaning of sanctions-removal. In the first place it becomes increasingly unconvincing to accept the argument that sanctions have been 'neutral'. Second, cumulative long-term effects must have been of grave consequence—and should primarily be seen in the sphere of the investment-employment mechanism. Thirdly, even if it is true, as the Standard Bank has claimed, that 'it is simply impossible to calculate the net impact of economic sanctions since 1965', it is clear that the impact has been negative in the long-term. Finally, the results provide a caution against facile claims that in the future sanctions-removal will be either inconsequential or, contrariwise, that the removal in itself presents the *fons et origo* for a future development solution.

IV SANCTIONS-REMOVAL AND POTENTIAL IMPACT

What then might the economic effects of sanctions-removal be? Here the answers seem to turn as much on the nature of the external removal *process* itself—its comprehensiveness, speed, timing, associated 'linkage effects' in the domestic economy, and internal policy readjustments—as on assumptions made about the *context* of the scenario within which these eventualities might conceivably take place.

The options

Various options could be considered ranging from the *maximalist* position of comprehensive sanctions removal *with* international recognition *plus* cessation of the war to far more modest changes involving various elements of these. For instance, some countries might hold to sanctions longer than others if the recognition issue is in dispute. Equally, cessation of the war and military de-escalation (including accompanying financial and economic restructuring) is unlikely to be a very short-term exercise. Then too, as with sanctions application so with removal will the new government's economic policy have a major impact on the outcome through their management of changed economic conditions.

Given these imponderables, and the difficulty of dealing with intermediate cases, it might seem worthwhile positing estimates for changes under the maximalist case. Others could be considered as different or scaled down versions of this option and can be approximated through a process of qualification to expected changes which could occur in major economic variables over the short and long-term.

Variables and possibilities over the short and long-term

Begin, firstly, by wishing the new state of Zimbabwe the 'best of British luck'—no drought and no other natural disasters for at least the first three years, 1980-83.[17] Also recognise though, that over a decade, on historical experience, one would have to admit at least two poor agricultural seasons. Then, too, ignore the likelihood that the world economy appears to be slowing down for 1980 and is probably going to experience higher inflation rates, both of which factors would squeeze Zimbabwe's balance of payments.

a) Visible trade

Now take external sector trade changes first and assume that an average 20 per cent discount benefit on trade values will fully accrue to the economy in 1980. On currently expected 1979 GDP levels (calculated as down about 2 per cent on real 1978 levels) and using an estimated 39 per cent trade/GDP ratio, this would yield around $175 million in *new* foreign currency earnings (1978 prices). The 1980 figure without sanctions might be a bit above this level. It can be noticed immediately that this might be on the high side. The 'recoverable component' of the trade discount may well be less than 20 per cent and not so easily secured in the first year since 'contract switching', on-going commitments in the pipeline, and bargaining would be involved. *Other* negative tendencies in commodity terms of trade are also conveniently being overlooked (and probably should not be, e.g. for oil). It also implies that export constraints (e.g. on transport capacity for bulk commodities) will not exist. To consider the full sum involved as an investment fund—a further step —would require acceptance of no increases in imported consumer goods components.

Over the longer term, it is more reasonable to anticipate an elimination of present middlemen margins as well as a better regional spread of imports and exports (more diversified away from the South African Customs Union Area).[18] Moreover, in this time-frame, sensible commodity composition changes on exports as well as a resurgence in exports and re-exports and higher values from non-monetary gold sales would also tend to push up the *net* visibles balance—provided that, as always, proper import controls (amended to meet new conditions) also applied. For the moment, however, stick with the $175 million estimate.

b) Invisibles

It is probable also that short-term and sustainable benefits could be secured on invisibles. Much of the possible turnaround on this item though will depend on regional transport and political conditions as well as the specific character of domestic policy (notably in the exchange control sphere). Under services, 'transit freight earnings' could rise a little with even greater throughput of Zambian/Zairean traffic. The gains might be small in the short-run since it is reported that already a large amount of Zambian traffic is routed through Rhodesia Railways. However, other consequences of economic re-integration with Zambia and adjacent economies must not be overlooked and in the long-term both trade and services benefits could be secured by Zimbabwe. 'Other transport earnings' might flow from a resumption of the country's role in regional airways networks. Net savings on foreign travel are also within the scope of effective exchange control policies; and, if it is assumed that Zimbabweans will in future be less inclined to spend funds abroad (though this may not hold for the short-term), then small gains could come on this item as well.

On the current account 'investment income' item, most historically negative trends have been connected to the corporate sector and dividend and interest payments. Thus future movements will be conditioned by a combination of state exchange controls (which are unlikely to be much altered for some years by any future government) and investor confidence. If sanctions-removal is perceived abroad to lead to growth deserving of further local re-investment, these flows might not expand in a negative direction. But to the extent that there is a continuation of hostilities, uncertainty about the role of specific private enterprises, and attempts to shift funds out of the potential influence of an untried government's grasp, then an increased 'bleeding' of funds could ensue. Moreover, the build-up of blocked funds arising from sanctions implies a future outflow on this item, the effects of which would depend upon debt re-scheduling arrangements, intergovernmental negotiations, and foreign exchange availability.

Movements under the 'personal sector' heading of investment income will largely reflect net balances on pension fund transactions. At present this is a difficult one to foresee and, although now small, it could conceivably add to negative flows. 'Government sector' balances will depend directly on what is decided now about the liquidation of external debt liabilities (a point discussed below).

The 'transfers' element of invisibles is a mixed bag. Historically it has been a small negative element in the invisibles outflow (at around 8 per cent in *net* terms, in 1978). It might be assumed that white net migration will continue to be negative at an indeterminate (possibly high) level in the short-run and this could be associated with sizeable outflows of monies. Some of these funds might be blocked by government policy. The size of outflows could reflect both a once-off migration at Independence as well as gradual running down in the numbers of whites left thereafter (from 240,000 in 1979). To a large extent, what happens in the early days will much depend on the effective control exercised by the Reserve Bank and the authorised dealers. Any precipitate action allowing 'capital flight' in the sphere would pose serious difficulties for the future since Zimbabwe will undoubtedly need foreign exchange for essential imports, let alone growth.

'Migrant workers remittances' are now probably not unimportant including as they do the large contract-specified flows from Zimbabwean mineworkers on South African gold mines (possibly worth as much as $8 million annually). Will Zimbabwe maintain this link? If Mozambique experience is a guide the answer is likely to be affirmative. Yet in the long-run the South African Chamber of Mines' labour demand strategy will certainly continue to dictate reduced dependence on all supplier states; and Zimbabwe, under independent government, may well see its longer-term status revised in this contract labour market as BLS countries (and, increasingly, South African 'Bantustans') take greater preference in the employers' hierarchy of suppliers. This aspect has more than foreign exchange implications since, while it is undoubtedly true that mining skills could return to Zimbabwe under a cut-off policy, so too would unskilled employment grow (by around 20,000 jobs).

Given all the aforementioned permutations (and deficiencies on data for gross flows), it is not easy to put a reliable figure on the changes expected in invisible items in a post-sanctions world, either in the short or long-term. But it is known historically that invisibles have always been negative. It is also known that this has become more so in recent years. Therefore one should be reasonably sanguine about the future.

On rather crude hypotheses, then, that the *most* favourable balance of payments position will be attained on all three separate invisibles items —by which is meant 'optimal' regional conditions, effective exchange control, no 'capital flight', savings on external freight costs, higher internal freight earnings, low rates of company dividend remittance abroad, continued sizeable contractee earnings, etc.—the net benefits to the balance of payments might be considered at 10 per cent, 15 per cent, and 20 per cent of the net 1978 figures for services, investment income, and transfers.[19] It should be stressed that these gains are quite arbitrarily assumed. Be that as it may, the effect would be to diminish the 1978 invisibles outflow of $163 million by around $18 million, resulting in a saving of 11 per cent in all. If the 1980 position is to be determined, again under earlier assumptions, this sum should be increased to a net benefit of (say) around $20 million. In the longer term there is no reason why a sizeable share of these savings could not be permanently built into the balance of payments structure.

From the current account side, then, on the very *best* assumptions a non-sanctioned 1980s economy could potentially have a sizeable surplus —anything up to $200 million. Much of this sum, moreover, might stand a fair chance of being diverted to investment. Once again, allowance for second-best conditions, 'slippage' in securement of the discount, leads and lags in transactions, as well as the adjustment difficulties of a new trade regime could see this sum more realistically in the $100 million range. Either way, it puts the Zimbabwean economy in a fairly strong growth position, more particularly so if capital account movements in this phase are positive. But will they be?

c) *Capital account transactions*
Again, one is working in the dark in making reliable estimations of net movements on capital account. Detailed data cease abruptly in 1972. Private capital flows are fickle. Public capital inflows will be a function of widespread political recognition as a pre-condition and well-known lead-time gestation difficulties will exist in converting both multi-lateral and bilateral commitments into actual disbursements.

Consider, first, *private capital movements*. Already today gross inflows exist. Net inflows are also managed by control exercised on gross outflows. Assuming the new government is disposed to new inflows, a question thus arises as to whether *fresh* private investment will in fact be attracted to Zimbabwe. Under the maximalist scenario the reply for the long-term would be affirmative. In the short-term, some hesitation could readily be forecast. Yet, there are presently some hundreds of foreign companies already *in situ* (accounting for as much as 60 per cent of productive capital stock) including some of the largest transnationals in the world.[20] This represents a large externally-held capital stock in the private sector. Since these have been by nature long-term investment commitments, TNCs *might* move quickly to consolidate and expand their operations, even to the extent of providing immediate external finance for activities under an uncertain economic regime. But many may well wait in the wings and not make immediate and massive financial commitments.

What will new government policy be towards TNCs, the impressive size of existing foreign capital stock, new investors, and the existing range and character of foreign corporate operations? These are major imponderables no less dependant on the composition of a new government as on its view of pragmatic necessities. Neither can be predicted here. However, if net private capital inflows are no smaller than were the average of the capital inflows of the 1974-1978 recessionary years (assuming it almost all represented non-public monies), one would anticipate around $27 million in net terms going through in 1980. On the other hand, this would be a low sum under economic conditions considered as very favourable by external companies. It should be realised therefore that this sort of inflow level could well be triple the sum of $27 million without great difficulty. The fact that TNCs could potentially quickly re-establish historic links, that Eurodollar credits could be easily secured against the country's debt position, and that supplier credits would be more easily secured under independence conditions, leads to the conclusion that a potential current account surplus would be supported by a capital account inflow. The implication to follow would be a direct build-up in reserves and higher investment levels in productive sectors than prevailed in the recent past.

Official capital inflows would add to the total flow. A situation of international recognition without sanctions and no war could signal major external concessional assistance availability in grant and loan form from major donors—DAC countries, bilateral and multilateral institutions, and diverse non-governmental sources. Assume a new government wanted these monies. If so, and even allowing for negotiation delays, lead-times, project identification difficulties, aid 'diversion', local costs of technical assistance, and so on, the end result could be greatly to strengthen the long-term balance of payments position. Import procurement options could radically alter and effective use and proper allocation of ODA across sectors and by income group could do much for economic reconstruction, social rehabilitation after the war, and output reflation with economic growth. No realistic figures can be put on this item now. But the character of possible changes need not be mistaken. Indeed, the longer-term possibilities would seem promising for Zimbabwe. Some new trade agreements might conceivably be linked to capital inflows, e.g. under Lomé II, should Zimbabwe at some point accede to that Agreement and obtain STABEX benefits and/or other flows from the EDF. An independent Zimbabwe would also ultimately be eligible for UNDP-funding with a quinquennial Indicative Planning Figure of no small magnitude. Access to **IBRD** and (possibly) **IDA** funds would over time add to these resources should Zimbabwe seek Bank membership as concommitantly would similar rights materialise if the new State joined the **IMF** to obtain access to **SDR** and credit facilities.

d) *The debt problem*

Up to this juncture, comment on debt obligations has been left aside. Special account needs to be taken of external debt liabilities. Payments on capital and interest have been frozen since 1966 for a large part of the external debt. Some 'secret or illegal' loans may have ben made and might have been covertly serviced. There is a measure of uncertainty on this score. What will a new government decide to do and in fact be capable of doing? Will it willingly inherit all the debt from an illegal regime? Will it negotiate with the Bank of England about meeting commitments to UK bondholders? Will the UK government and the IBRD require quick and early payment or will a debt repudiation and/or rescheduling exercise ensue as part of a package of sanctions-removal policies? If there is repudiation, even only in part, what ramifications might this have on private and official creditors?

Without answers to these points no simple calculations may usefully be made. But it is probably likely that some part of the past redemption and interest liabilities (estimated in total for the public sector at $150 million for pre-1965 borrowings and $250 million for post-1965) will be serviced in future and will represent a net outflow on the balance of payments.[21] Over 1965-78 net external borrowings amounted to $366 million, the volume and share of total external to internal borrowings falling over the period. Of total state debt of $1,150 million in 1978 only 8 per cent was external. On the other hand, new external debt contracting would not be difficult to envisage—dependent on development programmes, servicing capacity, supply availability, and ultimately credit ratings. The eventual outcome clearly affects both current and capital account positions.

e) *Output growth*

So far the examination has been based on identifying possible changes in the external sector as they might affect investment and financial resources prospects. The impression obtained is one of an economy in a position to finance increased imports, absorb new capital inflows, and build up foreign currency reserves. What does this mean in output growth terms? For a start, it should be accepted that the post-sanctions economy in 1980 would start with some excess capacity. But how much? There is no really reliable estimate available. Production is currently down in all principal sectors by varying degrees. Full capacity utilisation with presently aged capital stock might, however, be considered as related to (say) the ratio of wage employment levels now (around 990,000) as compared to the historical peak (1975=1,055,000), that is 6.2 per cent. Whilst this is a crude measure, based on modern sector conditions, it may not be too far off. Assume then that this capacity could be brought immediately into production and, in so doing, it eliminated the real output fall of −2 per cent for 1979 leaving a growth potential of around 3-4 per cent for 1980. Take the favourable balance of payments earlier postulated, which should allow for a bit more growth, and then deduct a portion for immediate reconstruction costs and non-directly productive needs (e.g. refugee resettlement, etc.) All in all, taking a growth-biased view, one might be left with a real growth in GDP for the first 'sanctions-free' year of around 3 per cent. (Doing the sums differently could of course give an inferior starting position.) Assume, furthermore, control over inflation and sustainability of this growth rate throughout the 1980s. Ignore, too, for the moment, any significant diversion of outlays for reconstruction beyond year one, as well as no adverse years for the primary sectors, and imagine an economy following a secular growth path. What would happen?

TABLE IV: *Zimbabwe: Effects of Hypothetical Growth Rates 1980–1990 (constant 1965 prices)*

	(1)	(2)	(3) Population (000) Annual Growth Rate	(4) GDP per head (dollars) GDP Growth	(5) GDP per head (dollars) GDP Growth
	GDP ($ millions) Annual Growth Rate				
	3%	5%	3.6%	3%	5%
1980	1,193.8	1,253.9	7,460	160.0	168.1
1981	1,229.6	1,316.5	7,729	159.1	170.3
1982	1,266.4	1,382.3	8,007	158.1	172.6
1983	1,304.3	1,451.4	8,295	157.2	174.9
1984	1,343.5	1,523.9	8,594	156.3	177.3
1985	1,383.8	1,600.1	8,903	155.0	179.7
1986	1,425.3	1,680.1	9,215	154.6	182.3
1987	1,468.0	1,764.1	9,547	153.7	184.8
1988	1,512.0	1,852.3	9,891	152.8	187.3
1989	1,557.0	1,944.1	10,247	151.9	190.3
1990	1,603.7	2,046.5	10,616	150.9	192.8

Source: Calculations based on CSO, *National Accounts and Balance of Payments of Rhodesia 1977* (Salisbury, 1978).

Note: The 1978 real GDP is taken (as per *Economic Survey of Rhodesia 1978*) at −3.6% of 1977 while 1979 is estimated at a level −2% below 1978 in real terms. Population growth rate annually taken at 3.6% as per *1969 Census* and *Monthly Digest of Statistics*.

In bland statistical terms, the results are found in Table IV where a 3 per cent growth path is compared with another, of 5 per cent secular increase in GDP, far more favourable and subject to even more stringent real world qualifications (all figures are in *constant 1965 prices*). With a 3 per cent path the historical GDP peak of 1974 is achieved once again only in 1985 (compare Table I here). The 1990 GDP level of $1,604 million is, however, still 36 per cent above 1978's performance.

But welfare at large is intimately connected to *per capita* levels and trends (see column 4). Under the 3 per cent growth regime, GDP per head falls slowly but surely over time—from a low of $160.6 in 1980 (itself below the 1965 level) to an even smaller $151 per head. In total, this would be a 5.6 per cent cut in average living standards over 10 years of positive but low GDP expansion. Under the 5 per cent growth path GDP rises to the historical peak by 1982. In this scheme the 1984 level exceeds the 1990 result for the 3 per cent growth path. Income per head moves consistently upwards—this being directly related to the annual 3.6 per cent population growth rate. Even so, the 1990 product per head of $192.8 still falls 13.7 per cent *below* the historical high of $223.6 (1974) even though it would stand 27.7 per cent in excess of the terminal result of 3 per cent growth model.

The argument thus far has been to examine the 'optimistic side' of calculations about the aftermath of sanctions removal. Yet there are, as have been identified, numerous obstacles to even the inferior growth path actually being realised as projected in the admittedly simple and rather deterministic model. The rudimentary contrast drawn, on the other hand, sharply portrays the critical impact which a particular rate of steady growth, or its non-attainment, might have on Zimbabwe's economic future. If optimistic consumptions are relaxed, what would happen—for example, if it took some years to 'turn around' the recession and induce a positive growth pattern? And more so, what if growth was not sustained over the full decade, if bad harvests diminished the assumed rate (especially in the vital, early years of the period), if skills scarcities constrained expansion, and if inflation cut real growth? The answer needs little elaboration, more especially for an economy recovering from sanctions distortion and war with structural unemployment and every sign of poverty amongst the vast majority of households.

f) *Investment*

The 'turnaround' from recession, and the prospects of sustained growth, can thus be seen as dependent heavily on what happens to net investment. Already it has been mentioned that some funds would in practice need to go towards capital stock replacement, to offset ageing equipment and to 'gear-up' the economy to protect productivity rates and international competitiveness. Monies would also be drawn off for relief, social rehabilitation, refugee assistance, and so on. While some of these outlays might be designed to have an investment component attached, for the most part they would be of a social consumption character even though they could be deemed absolutely necessary as expenditures against the budget. Moreover, the largest portion of this type of outlay would come in the early part of the 1980s, the very period when a strategic growth turnaround appears vital and the scale of which will have great compound effect on GDP trends.

No calculations have been made here of *additional* investment requirements above a 1979 level of $400 million and needed to sustain a steady 3-5 per cent growth path; but it is easy to foresee that these would have to be *at least* in the region of an additional $100 to $165 million in the first year, the amount rising over the decade on a steady basis, on the rather hopeful assumption that a very favourable capital-output ratio (say of 1.5, suggesting significant high capital utilisation and efficiency) applied.[22] This would put GFCF at around $500-565 million in year one. Any slippage in investment levels or efficiency of capital use would imply direct future costs in terms of lower output growth over the decade. In practice, average capital-output ratios are probably in the 2.5 range. So a sum greater than the amount mentioned would be needed. Moreover, the priority to be accorded employment expansion is only one of a number of possible reasons why even less favourable capital-output results might be allowed. A need for infrastructural outlays and allocation to services needs would similarly push the ratio upwards.

g) *Sectoral aspects*
It is worthwhile now highlighting briefly a few important sectoral conditions which may be affected by sanctions-removal.

Agriculture: In agriculture a critical immediate matter will be net domestic food supply (now negatively affected by the war), decline in commercial and peasant sector surpluses, continued food exporting prospects, and producer prices. The timing and process of sanctions lifting could also have a large effect on new plantings, crop finance availability, the restocking of herds, agricultural output growth (notably in tobacco, sugar and beef), and export returns. But, equally, all these matters will not be easily or instantly resolved; and a new government will have to implement some commitment to land reform and rural reconstruction both of which could have negative short-term output effects. Since some change in land tenure, ownership, landholding, and agricultural policy would seem inevitable in some form, it will matter a great deal just how effectively these policies are designed, implemented, and followed through, remembering here that 38 per cent of visible export earnings come from agriculture.

Manufacturing: In manufacturing as well there is undoubted excess capacity to be quickly brought on stream. This would come with a better availability of spares and imports. The 1978 level of output was a clear 10 per cent below 1974's. Zimbabwe's manufacturing sector, although protected, has a strong potential regional competitiveness. A key question will be the retention of its foothold in the South African market and possible expansion in trade to previously 'lost' markets (e.g. Zambia and elsewhere). If these two facets are simultaneously accomplished, and effective domestic demand flourishes, high growth rates could follow. Some 'trade diversion' from South Africa's traditional African export markets is also possible. But the pattern of manufacturing production itself could well alter if there is a demand shift to non-luxury production, a stress on capital goods sectors (e.g. metals and metal products), and selective revision to existing import substitution practices. Critical policy questions—concerning the role of the State, ownership and control over equity, and wage policy—could nonetheless possibly be in question and may well affect optimistic trends in the short-term.

Mining: In the mining sector important gains might also be foreseen. New investment would have long gestation periods and recovery in exploration would take time to yield results. But higher export prices, lower transport costs, and additional finance could stimulate short-term improvements. The mining output base is fortunately well diversified and potential increased linkages with manufacturing would not be difficult to realise with new finance directed to establish plants. The main commodities likely to benefit would be copper, nickel, chrome, and asbestos. Greater domestic coal use could itself help reduce the liquid fuels bill for all sectors. As with manufacturing, however, these enterprises are largely under TNC control. Consequently, new government relationships and policy in this sphere will be of the utmost importance. In particular, the large foreign companies will be looking for stable government, security on tax policies, dividend repatriation commitments, constraints on nationalisation tendencies, and possibly limited equity holdings by the state (say, through the Mining Development Corporation).

Services: These, generally defined, would tend to move in line with the overall level of economic activity. However, if income distribution patterns alter quickly, as they might, the nature of demand would change. New consumption patterns are probably most likely to be evidenced in public services, e.g. health, evaluation, and welfare provisions. Dependent on policy, it is not impossible to imagine a long-term build-up in the tourist sector—now well down on early 1970s levels. On the other hand, a necessary future choice between initial high investment rates and increases in disposable income and consumption outlays will have much to do with the particular success of sub-sectors and specific firms.

Construction: Sanctions lifting would re-stimulate construction output, especially under an expanded development programme. But skills constraints might prove a short-term bottleneck. Over time, however, this labour-intensive sector could provide an important stimulus to employment.

h) *Public sector*
Various imminent changes in public policy have been mentioned. So has the importance of policy responses for maximising the benefits from sanctions-removal. In the public sector itself, economic recovery will have a major impact on raising tax revenues. This should not be seen as excluding tax re-structuring, some of which is most likely. In general, a shift back from the indirect tax thrust of 1967-79 would seem on the cards. Higher corporate and individual rates would probably be relied upon to pick up the slack. At the same time, the relative size of the state sector has grown uninterruptedly since 1965. It is difficult to imagine this trend being reversed; indeed, with pressures for new initiatives, reconstruction policies as well as greater control, the likely direction to be anticipated is a more interventionist one. It will only be limitations of finance and deficit budgeting, with attendant inflationary consequences, as well as skills shortages (notably of exiled Zimbab-

weans), which are likely to impose the main immediate constraints on this trend. Nonetheless, many new programmes could find funding through the substitution of existing Votes and diversion of previously military outlays (now taking a 38 per cent slice of the $446 million budget). How far and how quickly the military element of state outlays is diminished will therefore be pertinent to growth over the long-term.

It might also be expected that price controls will continue—both to dampen expected inflationary tendencies as well as restructure relative prices. This will be of particular importance in ensuring containment of the damage caused by the currently high 16.5 per cent annual rise in import prices whilst the inflation rate sits in the 12 per cent range and has all the propensities for rising further. Part of the package to contain inflation will undoubtedly be a reversal of the rigid controls which promoted low interest rates in the past. This could be most visible at the long end of the market and on a discriminating basis by asset/sector dependent on new 'Central Bank' directives. Domestic liquidity would probably shrink under restrictive policies, high demand and greater controls likely to be placed over the four large foreign banks (Barclays, Standard, Grindlays, and Rhobank) which dominate the banking sector.

A far bigger set of questions revolve around retention of exchange rate parities, possible new linkages to the SDR or a 'currency basket', and Rand/dollar rates (dependent on implied de-linking from South Africa over time). Zimbabwe will not have wholly independent manoeuverability on this front. Exporters would like to see devaluation but in the short-term existing constraints on the export pipeline may well hold this possibility at bay. Yet, if inflation rises, South African trade links weaken, and new patterns quickly emerge, devaluation might follow in due course.

It would be no underestimate, then, to state that a new government is going to be considerably stretched on the policy side. There exist a whole battery of sanctions controls to be reconsidered and eventually dismantled where necessary (in the field of services, subsidies, taxes, minimum wages, labour, trade, banking, and prices). But no immediate lifting of import or exchange controls is to be expected. New policies will be needed to take their place. These do not come out of thin air. Coping with immense practical problems as well as a wide range of policy problems and reforms will thus stretch administrative capacity and efficiency. Not the least of these difficulties will be focused on new relationships with the private sector, e.g. in the spheres of credit, technology, skills utilisation, and investment. But perhaps this is labouring the obvious.

V CONCLUSIONS

What is the conclusion of all which has gone before? In essence the argument has been that through balance of payments and investment changes it is feasible to consider Zimbabwe's long-term future up to 1990 as being one which might set it on the road to recovery to past levels of income and growth. That is a highly tentative statement based as much on evidence as on hope.

The general conclusion has been heavily qualified in many ways not only because that is in the nature of economic analysis (or should one say economists). It is also because there *are* indeed many factors which could upset the apple-cart and the rose-tinted picture drawn of the post-sanctions economy, *viz.* the assumptions of comprehensiveness in sanctions-removal; full international recognition, speedy execution of the new policy (and not protracted negotiation); an associated and rapid cessation of hostilities; quick conversion of the economy from its war orientations; judicious domestic policy responses; an element of luck in not having to face serious natural disaster; no constraint on external financial flows and a discounting of world economic slowdown with higher international inflation; a high allocation of funds to investment; sustainability in the growth process, and disallowance of any negative effects (suggested by the Standard Bank) that political changes might create uncertainty which would possibly induce a large-scale 'skills drain'.

The broad conclusions drawn also tend to establish a position somewhat different from both the 'conventional' and 'official' wisdoms on sanctions-removal. In this paper the growth possibilities following sanctions-removal are acknowledged; it is a view built upon an interpretation that sanctions application in the past has indeed had serious results over the long-term. In short, sanctions removal matters. In fact, some benefits have already filtered through as a result of accelerated sanctions erosion. Yet unlike 'official' theses the view put here is a far more qualified perspective in relation to development prospects, at least in the 1980s.

There is a real need not to underestimate the structural effects of past and existing policy as well as some terrible consequences of the war. Chronic unemployment, landlessness, urban and rural poverty, inequality, and the high level of external influence in the economy—all of which have long been evident—will not dissolve merely through sanctions-removal. Nor will they wither simply with projection of past growth trajectories—no matter what their rate. After all, there is some doubt that Zimbabwe will emerge in 1990 any better off in pure economic terms than the position which prevailed at the peak of the 1974-75 boom. That is the rather sobering message to be considered *unless* growth rates (and all which higher rates imply) can be lifted well above 5 per cent per head in constant price terms over 1980-90.

One is aware also, however, that growth is not the sole criterion. It is not for this reason that the conflict has developed. At the same time, growth can be translated in some measure into employment and consumption levels, nutritional adequacy, and access to and quality of services. Some of these latter economic objectives might simply be achieved for the poorest groups through major distributional shifts. One genuine problem entailed in this outlook, however, is whether the consequences in a post-sanctions environment can be so managed as to yield the net improvements in absolute standards that are so desperately required for the bulk of the population.

NOTES

1. See *inter alia* various studies produced for the UNCTAD Economic and Social Survey of Zimbabwe (1979).
2. See T. Curtin and D. Murray, *Economic Sanctions and Rhodesia,* IEA Research Monograph, 12, 1967; C. C. Barnekov, 'Sanctions and the Rhodesian Economy', 3 *Rhodesian Journal of Economics* (March, 1969); R. T. McKinnell, 'Sanctions and the Rhodesian Economy', 7 *Journal of Modern African Studies* (1969).
3. See UN Reports of the Sanctions Committee (over the period 1968–78).
4. On oil see Martin Bailey and Bernard Rivers, *Oilgate,* (London, 1979).
5. Curtin and Murray, *op. cit.* and Barnekov, *op. cit.*
6. Curtin and Murray, *op. cit.,* 47.
7. Apologies to J. M. Keynes.
8. Barnekov, *op. cit.*
9. *Ibid.,* 73.
10. These calculations are based on a study by R. J. Davies, 'Rhodesia's Terms of Trade', 8 *Rhodesian Journal of Economics* (September, 1974). In 1966 exports fell 36 per cent and a 27 per cent fall in imports occurred—largely as a result of import controls.
11. See CSO, *Monthly Digest of Statistics* (Salisbury, 1973).
12. *Business Herald,* 14 June 1979.
13. Among those who have used such a figure see articles by Tony Hawkins, (London *Financial Times,* August/September 1974); also R. Riddell, 'Sanctions and the Zimbabwe Rhodesian Economy, (CIIR, London, mimeo, 30 July 1979).
14. Mr. J. Girdlestone (ARNI economist), for instance, has noted 'that although sanctions have had an effect they have never been crucial to our existence', *Guardian,* 7 July 1979.
15. The key assumptions stand out, *viz.* sanctions removal *will* involve an economic turnaround and growth *will* accelerate; and structural problems can *still* be addressed through growth alone (with minor adjustments).
16. See Standard Bank, 19 *Economic Bulletin—Zimbabwe Rhodesia* (September, 1979), in which it is noted that exports in 1978 were around $600 million whilst imports were $420 million. This would put combined imports and exports at higher than 39 per cent of GDP.
17. This is no simple jest. Witness the case of Mozambique where natural disasters following Independence had a serious negative effect on performance.
18. See UN Sanctions Committee Report (UN Doc. S/R529, 1977).
19. It is not at all certain that these benefits would pertain; or at least they could well result in different proportions—dependent on policies.
20. For details see D. G. Clarke, 'Foreign Companies and International Investments in Zimbabwe' (1980).
21. These sums would be equal to a whole year's imports (at least 1974 levels). There would thus be no possibility of instant repayment.
22. Higher capital-output ratios increase the amount of investment needed. Lower efficiency of utilisation does the same. Sectoral variations in the ratio also exist. Hence investment patterns will have a direct bearing on the overall return. The nature of investments (i.e. long or short-run, gestation periods, etc.) need also to be taken into account. For these reasons, assumptions used here are simplifying ones. The analysis should be qualified accordingly.

Political Scenarios and Their Economic Implications

by

Richard Hodder-Williams

University of Bristol

I

Prophesying about the future in Africa has normally been a hazardous occupation; prophesying about the future of Zimbabwe at this particular time is more hazardous than usual. While the demise of formal white political domination is manifestly at hand, it is by no means clear what this means for the economic, social, or political evolution of the country. The outcome of the Lancaster House Conference remains uncertain; the responses of Zimbabweans to its eventual outcome are unknown; the future involvement of peoples and governments outside Zimbabwe continues a matter of speculation; these uncertainties must inhibit all but the bravest, or foolhardy, from attempting to predict the future. Yet, it is important to look into that future with a clear eye, to spell out unequivocally the sorts of forces which will mould the new Zimbabwe; to rely on a touching faith that virtue and victory go hand in hand may well be the prelude to bitter disappointments and dissensions which could be avoided.

In constructing my schema, the building blocks are my assumptions; it is the sum of these assumptions which provides the thrust of my argument. They should, therefore, be made as explicit as possible. The first block, and a veritable cornerpiece to the edifice, is the assumption that, though economics and politics are analytically separable, they are inextricably intertwined in the real world, each feeding on the other, and each influencing the other. Previous speakers have, with great restraint, focused on the economic dimension of Zimbabwe's future, but they would, I know, be the first to admit that economic policies will be a function of the political forces, just as I will argue that the political direction of future governments in Zimbabwe will be affected, but not determined, by economic factors. The rationale for this particular talk is that different political futures may produce different economic consequences. Which political future will, in the short term, predominate depends on the outcome of the present talks at Lancaster House. I do not pretend to know what the detailed outcome of these will be; but clearly some assumption must be made.

My second assumption is that the finer detail of the Independence Constitution is not of intrinsic importance. There are, I think, good historical

reasons for taking this view. For all the care and time lavished on independence constitutions by Colonial Office officials in the course of dismembering
Britain's African empire, they have shown little propensity to survive.
Constitutions in any cases are merely pieces of paper and derive their controlling power only from a nation's volutary acceptance of the legitimacy of
that power. Independence constitutions were, furthermore, designed more
to ease the path towards the goal of independence than to arrange an
enduring distribution of power in the new state. Certainly independent
African states have found little difficulty, and shown less embarrassment, in
recasting the formal rules to fit the local alignment of power more accurately.
Usually this has been achieved through the civilian political apparatus;[1]
sometimes, as in Nigeria, it has needed military intervention. Both
possibilities must be borne in mind in considering Zimbabwe's future;
in the short term, however, I assume that the civilian authorities will dominate
this inevitable process of recasting. It would be naive to imagine that
constitutions play no part in delineating the distribution of power or have
no effect on the outcome of the political battle; but my own view is that any
constitution bequeathed to Zimbabwe, even one with quite rigid safeguards
for minorities, will not long survive.

Far more significant, however, are the arrangements through which the
next government of Zimbabwe accedes to power. It is this transitional period
which will profoundly affect the future. The argument now, as I see it,
is over who will control the formal apparatus of state power and it is a
control which is seen by all participants to embody genuine power. To
the victor in any forthcoming election go the spoils. And, in a country
where there are no traditions of active mass parties, no loyalties built
up over a succession of elections, and no history of open political debate,
where furthermore, the electorate is displaced, emotions run high, intimidation of one sort or another is endemic, and some major political movements
have little organisation on the ground, the precise conditions surrounding
any election take on an added importance. If a new government is to be
widely recognised as legitimate and granted the cloak of authority without
which power is largely sterile, the arrangements for the pre-independence
election must be a matter of central concern. My own view is that the
United Kingdom should take imaginative steps to ensure that the government
in the interim period between Lancaster House and elections wins the trust
of all participants. It well may need a major reversion to colonial form,
to a genuine Executive Council on which a number of imperial appointees
sit, before the necessary impression of disinterested objectivity can be
realised. I do not see, for example, why a temporary Council consisting of an
appointed Governor, appointed Secretaries for Finance, Internal Affairs,
and Justice (perhaps drawn from Commonwealth figures such as the former
Chief Justice of Tanzania, P.T. Georges) and appointed unofficial members
drawn from the competing political parties could not be set up. Be that as
it may, another of my building blocks, my assumptions, is that the 'transitional
phase' holds the major key to the future. It will not only produce the next
government; it will have a significant effect on the legitimacy and authority
of that government.

What, then, are the possible scenarios? Scenario I envisages an unsuccessful Lancaster House Conference (unsuccessful in the simple sense that the three participating parties fail to sign an agreed set of final documents) and a bilateral agreement between Britain and the Salisbury government. Scenario II envisages a successful conference and an ensuing election in which the forces of the Patriotic Front prove victorious; this I have divided into Scenario IIa and IIb to suggest that a Patriotic Front victory may either usher in a period of radical reforms and major structural change to the Zimbabwean economy, or, on the contrary, be merely a prelude to an essentially reformist administration. Scenario III envisages success at Lancaster House and an ensuing election in which Bishop Muzorewa prevails; I have not thought it necessary to subdivide this scenario into radical and reformist alternatives. Scenario IV envisages, once again, success at Lancaster House, but an election in which no single party emerges as the victor and no coalitions are established. I do not want at this stage to indicate in any way which seems the most likely; as far as success or failure at Lancaster House is concerned, instant agonising is a waste of precious time, for we shall shortly know the truth, one way or the other.

II

Before we pursue these scenarios further and flesh them out substantially, it is necessary to return again to my building blocks. One of the fundamental assumptions underlying the whole of my analysis has been that the rulers of Zimbabwe will be faced with choices. Earlier speakers in this series, when they addressed themselves to possible solutions for the problems they examined, implicitly assumed that it mattered greatly who occupied the seat of power. In other words, however constrained by the international economic system Zimbabwe may be, the possibility of different forms of development and different paths towards that development was generally conceded. Nobody would be so simple-minded, surely, as to imagine that any state in Africa these days can realistically hope to follow an autonomous path of development, entirely unaffected by the markets and values of the rest of the world; likewise, nobody, surely, thinks so lowly of the calibre of African leaders that they are portrayed as nothing more than puppets directed and determined from without. There is certainly no universal agreement even on a definition of development itself, so that the goals to which future leaders aspire may well differ greatly.[2] Whatever conception of development prevails, there will of necessity be some limits to what can, and what cannot, be done; precisely what these limits prove to be depends not only upon external forces, but on the commitment and resilience of internal forces.

Any new government, however, will be faced by internal as well as external constraints. Our previous speakers have invoked many of them. The general threnody of earlier weeks must have filled most observers with a humbling realisation of the enormity of the tasks facing the politicians. Before I add to that threnody, it is perhaps pertinent to observe that what is a problem to one observer is a given to another, that what seems of central importance to one political persuasion is merely an unfortunate fact of life to another. Consequently, the sorts of problems different governments will want to 'solve' will vary and so, also, will their likelihood of success. In addition, however, to the issues of land, unemployment, egalitarian development, the control of capital investment, and so forth to which attention has already been drawn, I would like to stress yet further factors of importance. The dislocations forced upon Zimbabweans by the internal war have been massive; any government, whatever its political hue, will be faced immediately with the cost of relocating peasant families, restarting productive agriculture in their own homes, and integrating the thousands of refugees back into a social system with the internal strength to endure. On top of this, the basic infrastructure of much of rural society has been destroyed and it will take time, and money, and dedication to rebuild the trading networks, the administrative structure, the communications, and the educational system. Another of my assumptions, then, is that any future government will be forced to devote much of its initial energies to undoing the ravages of war; since all but the most outrageous of African leaders have been nationalists first and foremost and have genuinely desired to provide above all what they believe to be best for their people, I see this as being a fundamental priority for whatever successor government emerges.

The concentration on immediate problems and general limitations on freedom of choice brings me to my next assumption. Any government will be *dirigiste*. The governors of Rhodesia became increasingly *dirigiste* and their attempts to control more and more of the economic and social life of the country provides the basic conditions for any future government to continue the centralising tendencies. The immediate seriousness of a multitude of matters will also encourage the use of directives and the lack of political traditions which permit exceptions and mavericks will strengthen this general tendency. If there are any lessons to be learned from the rest of independent Africa (and I think there are many), one is that governments seek power in order to use it and do not feel embarrassed about exercising that power. The difference between future governments in Zimbabwe will not lie in the method of exercising power so much as in the direction to which it is put.

I have so far talked somewhat abstractly about governmental power as though the future of Zimbabwe's economy was merely a function of governmental will on the one hand and internal and external constraints on the other. To some extent, this is the truth, but it is far too cavalier a way to treat the constituent parts of that simple equation. I would break it down into six interconnected forces, each of which provides a building block for my schema, and each of which must be the subject of explicit comment.

The first of the parts is the future government and its close advisers. How the years to come are foreseen depends very much upon each individual observer's estimation of the ideology, skills, and political following of the potential leaders. I do not want to enter too deeply into this minefield, but it is, nonetheless, a minefield which must be traversed. I shall step daintily by avoiding comments on specific individuals and by making general points drawn from my study of politics in general and of African politics in particular. First, it is often easy to be seduced by the rhetoric of politicians just as it is easy to be misled by them. The genial buffoonery of an Idi Amin can be a poor indicator of the policies of an Amin's rule; the words of Jomo Kenyatta, whom Governor Renison once called the 'leader to darkness and death', or of Kamuzu Banda, the radical *bête-noir* of conservatives twenty years ago, belie their future actions. Nor have the present competitors for power in Zimbabwe always spoken consistently or, indeed, acted consistently. Political speeches tend to perform political functions and can only be fully appreciated in their particular contexts.[3] Second, if the lessons of independent Africa are of relevance, the bourgeois tendencies of political leaders are hard to ignore. In part, of course, this is because the struggle for independence is often a struggle to inherit an existing state, already evolving on the model of its imperial master; in part, it is a comment on human nature, on human fallibility perhaps, but history does not belie the view that most people believe in accepting the opportunity to be bourgeois if it is offered rather than turning it down. Third, the new government will be faced, as I have said, with very immediate problems; one of them may well be the recasting of the formal constitutional rules. The experience of East and Central Africa suggests that this can be done within the inherited political structures, but that it occupies politicians' time to a considerable degree. In other words, the time available for restructuring the economy may be limited by more immediate and apparently pressing concerns. Fourth, it should not be forgotten that political leaders are subject to political pressures from within their own ranks and to political calculations about potential support for their programmes. It is for all these reasons that I have felt obliged to think in terms of both Scenarios IIa and IIb.

The second constituent part of my simple equation is the numerous band of middle level political workers and administrators without whom no party can affectively function and no government successfully rule. These crucial individuals are also nationalists; they, too, differ ideologically; but they tend to have a less sophisticated understanding of politics, a less developed array of conceptual tools to manage the political world. They normally divide into two groups, those who see the end of imperial rule as a chance to inherit the colonial state and those who slavishly follow the dicta and person of their party's leader. Both can provide formidable problems to governments. In Zimbabwe, my assumption is that both groups are well represented, but that the former, what I shall call the aspiring inheritors, form the majority. Certainly, there are already considerable vested interests in the country which will challenge a radical reduction in their existing positions of standing, let alone attempts to demote them. Business-men, head teachers, professionals of various kinds are already numerous and the last stages of the internal war have increased their numbers and their self-importance. This middle class which has newly acquired relative affluence is a political force not without spokesmen among the nationalist leadership. Furthermore, the considerable number of exiled Zimbabweans who will wish to return to their homeland are likely to strengthen the forces which prefer, let us say, an incipient Kenya to an incipient Tanzania. And there will in the short term be many openings in the bureaucracy and the parastatal organisations once independence comes to Zimbabwe; white emigration, statist philosophy, and the dirigiste ethos will see to that. It is, of course, true that in terms of high level manpower Zimbabwe will be much better placed than most other former British colonies in Africa, but technical qualifications are rarely substitutes for responsibilities borne and experience learned. The Zimbabweans who have those additional qualifications from employment outside Zimbabwe will add strongly to the internal forces favouring the reformist options.

There *will* be others, those who have been promoted within the exile movements themselves, those who have suffered long in detention, those who have intellectualised the need for profound change in an independent Zimbabwe. The politicisation of the war should not be ignored, but the permanent control exercised by radical, and articulate, guerilla leaders in the rural areas has not been great. There has been little repetition of FRELIMO's involvement in the daily life of northern Mozambicans in Zimbabwe, so that I tend to argue against those who foresee a radicalised peasantry and a determinedly progressive cadre of potential leaders. The strength of these progressive forces lies not in their numbers but in their commitment and their contact with fellow progressives at the centre; if their leading spokesmen fail to obtain central and influential positions in the new state, they are unlikely to play a determining part in an independent Zimbabwe.

The third constitutent part of the equation is the ordinary people of Zimbabwe. I would make two points about these nearly seven million inhabitants. First, the lessons of Africa indicate that their political role is greatest in those systems where a transformation of the economic and social system is intended. In the more conservative, reformist states, the fact of independence itself, the concomitant relaxation of racial discrimination, the symbolic and short-term advantages accruing to them, and the concern of the leaders themselves to concentrate their attentions elsewhere results in a measure of depoliticisation. However, and this is the second point, when governments do attempt to construct a new society in the rural areas, they face particular problems of support and cooperation. Reformist governments, in short, do not grant a greater relevancy to the peasantry than is required by their need for continuing labour and a successful subsistence sector; radical governments must see the peasantry as peculiarly relevant, since it is in the rural areas that a start in any fundamental alteration of the system must be made. Such governments are caught in a double bind. Too much *dirigisme* can be counter-productive; but too great a grant of autonomy, as has happened in Ethiopia, deprives the centre of that control necessary for a unified and coherent strategy of change. Of course, in the space of a couple of minutes, it is impossible to do justice to the complexities of the rural sector, let alone consider the intricacies of the urban sector. But the relevance of what I have said is simply this: economic policies require support from large numbers of individuals, but conventional liberal ones will involve little change in basic life styles; by contrast, radical economic policies not only need positive contributions from large numbers of individuals, they can also generate a focus for opposition.

The fourth constituent part of the equation are the gunmen. There are in affect five armies operating on the current Zimbabwe/Rhodesia stage, armies which are equipped with a wide range of military hardware. A cease-fire may put an end to organised violence between the Patriotic Front and the Salisbury government; it will not necessarily disarm their members nor put an end to private armies. In any power equation, groups with guns cannot be ignored, so that some assumptions about their behaviour must be made. In the short term, the prognostication can only be a pessimistic one. It is not simply that war brutalises and a peculiarly nasty war must brutalise many of its active participants, whatever sense of moral rectitude supports them; but a prolonged war creates a class of person for whom the civilian life is virtually unknown and often without attraction.[4] One should not, therefore, under-estimate the potential cost, financial and human, or the undermining of confidence in the government by outsiders and insiders as a result of continuing violence in Zimbabwe. In the longer term, the military, as the repository of armed force, will always be a possible alternative to a civilian regime, especially if its economic policies fail and its allocation of scarce resources is widely perceived as overly partisan. In the short term, clearly, the existence of armed men committed to the support of individual leaders will do little to ease the transition over the next few months; but elections will only be seen as free and fair if firm control is exercised over their activities, a control which a Governor, whatever his formal powers, will not be able adequately to perform without the support of armed forces under his command.

The fifth constituent part of the equation are the white people of Zimbabwe. Assumptions about their behaviour is critical, as is evident from what our earlier speakers have said. However, it would be a mistake to treat them as a monolithic whole, for they can be distinguished along lines which are significant for any evaluation of their future actions. I would stress four categories, the farmers, the professionals, the administrators (both civil and military), and the skilled and semi-skilled workers. Rhodesia has always been a country of impermanent white residence and perhaps half the present white population were not residents of Rhodesia when the Rhodesian Front first came to power. These comparatively recent immigrants tend to occupy the lower rungs of the white economic system and are the most likely to leave the country. Such an exodus might indeed be of positive benefit to the new Zimbabwean leaders, since it is precisely the kind of jobs these people hold down which other Zimbabweans are able and ready to take up. The other groups would prefer to stay, apart from some civil servants who are recent immigrants and those, like the senior Justices, who have been intimately involved in defending the dominant position of whites in Rhodesia since 1965. Clearly such men should be encouraged to leave. In some ways, this would ease the task of a successor government, since the segregatory practices of the past have inevitably left in the hands of the whites that part of the economy responsible for foreign earnings and the surplus necessary for governments' social policies as well as a disproportionate quantity of high level skills, technical knowledge, and general experience of the country's internal operations and, perhaps of special significance in the short term, external relations. Continuing to rely on such people, however, obviously detracts from the exercise of a fully independent black government; but this is essentially a political problem.

A massive and immediate transference of ownership, of land or manufacturing capital, would accelerate the exodus of the leaders of the most productive sectors of the economy. This exodus will be encouraged also by the availability of compensatory payments, which might tempt waverers to leave. An essentially reformist government would produce the least dislocation; a radical government intent on weakening the white hold on economic power would almost certainly exacerbate an already uncertain situation. Since, however, many whites are more deeply entrenched in Rhodesia than their counterparts were in Mozambique or Angola, the likelihood of an immediate and massive exodus of farmers, mining engineers, and professionals seems less; they have too much capital invested in the country and aspire to life styles requiring considerable resources. Only if very generous payments lured them positively away or anarchy and major attempts at expropriation pushed them away would many of them leave. In short, therefore, a peaceful transition to reformist rule would probably cause the loss of 80,000 or so whites from the current figure of about 240,000 within the first year; a bloody transition to radical rule would result in 200,000 leaving. My guess is that an intermediate figure will prove to be the more likely, with the professionals, most highly skilled technicians, and farmers providing the bulk of those remaining.

The sixth constituent part are the outsiders. To treat this part of the equation with the sophistication that is its due is impracticable this evening. But any estimation of Zimbabwe's political future, as of its economic future, must consider such factors as the world economy (declining). the propensity for transnational companies to invest or otherwise, the likelihood of South African economic or physical retaliation, the readiness and ability of Mozambique and Zambia to increase trade, or, in the event of a breakdown in the current negotiations, to continue military support to the Patriotic Front, the World Bank's eagerness to make loans and the terms on which such loans would be made, the ability of the rest of the world to absorb emigrants and provide skilled manpower to replace that which may be lost. In this respect Zimbabwe is not much different from other independent African countries short of indigenous capital and manpower and dependent on the outside world for markets. Because of the country's visibility and its potential strategic importance, however, I guess that governmental aid to the country may well be substantial. Although the ideological colour of its government may affect private investments, this may well not much influence governmental assistance.

The equation can thus be amended. The political future of Zimbabwe will be a function of its leaders' choice, its middlemen's aspirations, its people's support, the gunmen's cooperation, the white people's reactions to the new dispensation, and outside involvement. I have presented the permutations in a Table. Some initial comments are in order. First, I have indicated a net response for each of the constituent parts of my equation to make clear that reality is likely to be much more complex than the neat categorisation indulged in here suggests. Second, I have not weighted each of the constituent parts, although in my closing comments I will indicate, if only implicitly, my own judgement about relative weights. Third, I have defined 'success' as objectively as possible, namely the achievement of economic goals set by the government of the day in Salisbury. It need hardly be stressed that what one set of political leaders would describe as success is not necessarily what I, or indeed any of you, would also call success.

Net Support for Government (unweighted)

SCENARIOS

		I	IIa	IIb	III	IV
V	Leaders	0/−	+/0	+	+/−	—
A						
R	Middlemen	0/−	0	+	+/0	—
I						
A	Followers	0	0	+	0	0/−
B						
L	Gunmen	—	0/−	0/−	0/−	—
E						
S	Whites	0/−	—	+/0	+/0	—
	Outsiders	—	+/−	+	+/?0	0/−
	Net Support or 'success'	—	?+/−	+	+/?−	—

III

In setting up this matrix, in positing the variables that must be considered, I have attempted to cover most reasonable possibilities without passing judgement on the likelihood of any one possibility. The time, however, has come to give values to the variables of which my equation is composed and to enter the fraught thicket of personal judgement. For what it is worth, therefore, I will briefly indicate my own estimation of the likely future, taking each of my original scenarios in turn. (The plus, zero, and minus symbols indicate respectively positive, neutral, and negative values of support by different sections of the community for the government of Zimbabwe as established under a variety of scenarios. Where two values are given, the first assumes a transitional phase which produces a government widely seen as legitimate, the second assumes a transitional phase about which there are serious reasonable grounds for complaint.)

In Scenario I, a bilateral agreement is assumed. The African leadership will continue to be divided and the struggle of the Patriotic Front will go on;

the war will continue; the middlemen inside Zimbabwe will weaken in their support for the Muzorewa government; the common man will in public acquiesce while privately shifting support further towards the Patriotic Front; the armed gunmen will continue to fight although the Salisbury forces will be weakened by white emigration, black desertion, and increased acts of personal viciousness consequent upon increased desperation; the whites will accelerate their emigration; outside forces will on balance ensure both the survival of the Salisbury government and the continuing strength of the guerilla forces. Within a comparatively short space of time there will probably be some form of rapprochement after which a new government will be faced with the consequences of still greater ravages of war, a more dislocated economy, and a more disturbed population. The economic wellbeing of all but a small number of people will have deteriorated, but the prospects for a radical reconstruction of the country's economy and society will be enhanced. In this last respect, it is, I think, important to compare the situation facing Samora Machel in Mozambique when a massive exodus of whites left most of the estates and the productive agriculture sector untenanted; in such a *tabula rasa* and in a country with few indigenous vested interests, the opportunities for social and economic engineering are at their best.

Scenario II envisages a victory for the Patriotic Front at the polls. The African leaders would accept this; the middlemen would work for the new administration although they would in all probability exert pressure against too radical an equalising economic policy; the common man would accept the new government and would eagerly support some radical policies, such as land redistribution, but might react against too many restraints on the market economy or limitations on upward mobility; the gunmen would not wholeheartedly embrace such a development, since some members of an integrated armed force would watch the government with suspicion while others, outside the formal confines of the regular army, would develop into banditti, settling political scores, aggrandising themselves, and generally disrupting the even tenor of life in townships and rural areas. The whites would react variably, the majority seeking ways to leave if the radicalism of the Patriotic Front's rhetoric was turned into reality while many would stay under a reformist government; outside forces would tend to assist the new leaders, except that a radical government would find international capital and the Republic of South Africa distinctly less helpful than a reformist government. On balance, therefore, a IIb Scenario would, in so far as the possibilities inherent in Zimbabwe's economy allow, provide the environment for what the essentially reformist politicians would see as a successful economic policy; a Scenario IIa, however, would find itself perpetually struggling against forces, both inside and outside the country, intrinsically antagonistic to the leaders' aims.

Scenario III envisages a victory for Muzorewa after a tripartite agreement. The leaders here would, if the election was accepted as freely conducted, accept the result, though they would campaign against the successor government more strongly and with greater external support than Muzorewa is likely to under Scenario II; the middlemen would be divided initially, but would over time lend their support and skills to the new government; a majority of the common people would also accept the new leaders, which is hardly surprising given the scenario's assumption that Muzorewa had won; the gunmen would be a destabilising influence for the same reasons that they provided a problem under both versions of Scenario II; many of the whites would leave but many would stay, notably the farmers, professionals, and highly paid skilled technicians; outsiders would, on balance, lend considerable support to the new government, resources being made available in greater quantity and with greater readiness than under any other scenario. On balance, therefore, this Scenario, like IIb, would be generally accepted internationally but would, in its own economic terms, probably be more successful than any other.

Scenario IV envisages an election which no party won. This implies a split in the Patriotic Front between an essentially radical ZANU faction and a more pragmatic ZAPU faction. The possibilities in this case are extremely varied. One alternative is a coalition government, presumably between Mr Nkomo's ZAPU and Bishop Muzorewa's ANC. Then the responses outlined under Scenario III become applicable; indeed, external support as well as internal support is likely to be at its highest. I have, however, not accounted for this eventuality in the Table, but have taken Scenario IV to represent a situation of future intransigence between the various factions' leaders. If no coalition between the leaders proves possible, the country will be plunged again into political turmoil, with all three rival factions resorting to intimidation and violence to strengthen their position should a fresh election be called; the middlemen will, seeing the lack of reconciliation among their patrons, calculate carefully where their self-interest lies and throw themselves for the most part wholeheartedly into support of whoever they believe will prove victorious; for the common man, caught in the bitter infighting between the factions, alienation from the political process as a whole will probably increase; the gunmen will in part continue their former activities; the whites will continue to emigrate; outside powers will attempt, as best they can, to bring the warring groups round a negotiating table and to lend aid, moral and financial, to their chosen favourites. In this pessimistic scenario, clearly the economic potentiality of Zimbabwe in the short run is not good.

In many ways these scenarios are dispiriting. Neither the imaginative ideas for land reform and industrial development to which Roger Riddell and Colin Stoneman drew attention nor the hopeful possibilities for productive investment opened up by an improving balance of payments, outlined by Duncan Clarke, are likely to occur. Why not? Obviously, in two of my scenarios a continuing struggle for power militates against policies that require strong governments operating in a climate of supportive enthusiasm. In the other scenarios, I have tended to give considerable weight to what I may call 'drag factors'. Interventionist policies are always the most difficult to carry out and require strong governments with reserves of affection and commitment; radical reconstruction requires committed leadership, loyal and convinced lieutenants, and a friendly external environment; an explicitly equalitarian economic policy needs a degree of self-abnegation rarely found among elites. The combination of these factors seems unlikely to me.

Furthermore, there will be forces positively antagonistic to too egalitarian an economic policy, and many of these will be internal—higher paid miners, for instance, as has happened in Zambia, or the 'aspiring inheritors', as I have referred to others—as well as the external pressures from officials and unofficials alike. Nor can the consequences of the internal war on the spirit of cooperation be ignored. Although the aftermath of the Nigerian Civil War witnessed a remarkable, if in some respects uncomfortably easy, reconciliation (uncomfortable given the appalling suffering inflicted upon ordinary Nigerians at the behest of their political masters), there is no guarantee that this would happen inside Zimbabwe—or, indeed, between some of Zimbabwe's neighbours and certain successor regimes. Certainly the actions of nationalists have historically often been the subject of personal rivalries, bitter recriminations, and a sad lack of the spirit of cooperation and reconciliation.

Of central importance, given the magnitude of the tasks ahead, is a government that is not divided within itself nor distrusted by significant sections of the population. In this latter respect, the role that 'tribal' loyalties will play is clearly going to be of considerable significance.[5] Although the executives of the various political groups may draw their membership from a wide range of 'tribal' bases, the general perception of their national basis will not necessarily run parallel to this nationally representative leadership. Not only do individuals believe that certain groups are given preferential treatment because of their 'tribal' origins, but the leaders themselves often appeal to 'tribal' identity to consolidate their own political positions.[6] Although I am more optimistic than many in my belief that Zimbabwe will not immediately be riven by 'tribal' discord, it would only be sensible to put into any equation about the future the distinct possibility that both personal and 'tribal' rivalries will seriously impede the creation of a strong, unified, and committed government.

On balance, the likelihood of a strong government emerging which unifies the various peoples and ideological strands in Zimbabwe is not, alas, very high. So the dominant forces in the new Zimbabwe, as I see it, will be nationalist, statist, partially elitist, internally divided, and committed to a traditional notion of what development is and to traditional paths to reach it. From the point of view of Zimbabwe, reformism will predominate; from the imperial power's point of view, the so-called neo-colonial route to development will be chosen.

If we cast our eyes a little further forward and we assume that a tripartite agreement has produced a government which is widely seen as legitimate, perhaps one final point can be made. I would expect to see a consolidation of power in the hands of the victorious party as processes familiar in other African states begin to augment the power and standing of the government. A pincer movement, from the villages requesting their opposition members to join the governing party and from the elites who see patronage and resources being allocated disproportionately towards the friends of the governing party, will increase the nationwide support given to whichever party proves victorious in the 1980 election.[7] In other words, although the early months of Independence may well be much taken up in consolidating power and attempting to deal with the immediate problems thrown up by the fighting and the electioneering, within a short space of time it is likely that the successor government will have become more established and more firmly based. When that is the case, the hard decisions that may be needed to ensure that resources are allocated where they are needed rather than where the political pull is strongest will be more easily made. If the world recession is then over and animosities of the war years have largely been lain to rest, the prospects for a flourishing, though neocapitalist, economy may be good.

My fundamental point, therefore, is that the transitional phase will be crucial. If it is handled properly, if there is a genuine cease-fire, if the new colonial administration is seen by all sides to act in an even-handed manner, if the opportunity for the various factions to campaign is fully provided, then the new government will enjoy the authority that flows from legitimacy and the people of Zimbabwe will have a commitment to that government. But a botched election, hastily organised and carried out at the height of the rainy season, will provide the ideal conditions for a losing Patriotic Front to argue, perfectly plausibly, that the election was not free and fair.[8] In these circumstances, the British Government may imagine they have sloughed off their residual colonial responsibilities, but the future of Zimbabwe will still lie in the balance and peace will not come to that strife-torn land. The deep responsibility for ensuring that the proper conditions are met lies with the United Kingdom government and its Commonwealth friends on the one hand and the leaders of the competing factions on the other. The responsibility for choosing the successor government lies with the people of Zimbabwe. How they will choose remains an unknown quantity.

NOTES

1. Kenya provides an excellent example of this (as do both Tanzania and Zambia). See, for instance, Y. P. Ghai and J. P. W. B. McAuslan, *Public Law and Political Change in Kenya* (Nairobi, 1970) and H. W. O. Okoth-Ogendo, 'The Politics of Constitutional Change in Kenya since Independence, 1963–69', 71 *African Affairs* (1972), 9–34.

2. For a recent, and distinctly relevant, discussion of this, see Anne Phillips, 'The Concept of "Development",' 8 *Review of African Political Economy*, (1977), 7–20.

3. Christopher Clapham, 'The Context of African Political Thought', 8 *Journal of Modern African Studies* (1970), 1–13.

4. War may sometimes appear ennobling, but the few first-hand accounts of this civil war, the atrocities committed by both sides, the reputation of the Selous Scouts, and so on convince me that many personal crises and collective memories have been created which will hinder further the already extremely difficult task of intergroup accommodation.

5. 'Tribalism' is a difficult concept to apply to Rhodesia. Two language groups (the ChiShona speakers, covering about 80 per cent of the population and SiNdebele speakers, covering about 12 per cent) dominate, but divisions within the ChiShona speakers are also significant in some circumstances. A useful map and comment is Nicholas Ashford, 'The Crucial Choice Before Zimbabwe-Rhodesia', *Times*, 26 November 1979.

6. See Nelson Kasfir, 'Explaining Ethnic Political Participation', 31 *World Politics* (1978–9), 365–88; R. Molteno, 'Cleavage and Conflict in Zambian Politics: a study

in sectionalism', in W. Tordoff (ed.), *Politics in Zambia* (Manchester, 1974), 62–106. For a critique of the modern concept, see Archie Mafeje, 'The Ideology of Tribalism', 9 *Journal of Modern African Studies* (1971), 253–61.

7. Perhaps the best example of this pincer is drawn from post-independence Uganda. See C. T. Leys, *Politicians and Politics* (Nairobi, 1967) and G. F. Engholm and A. A. Mazrui, 'Crossing the Floor and the Tensions of Representation in East Africa', 21 *Parliamentary Affairs* (1967–8), 137–54.

8. The sorts of problems that may arise have already been rehearsed in the April 1979 elections. See: Viscount Boyd of Merton, *Report to the Prime Minister on the Election held in Zimbabwe-Rhodesia in April 1979* (mimeo, Conservative Central Office); Claire Palley, *Zimbabwe-Rhodesia: should the present government be recognized?* (Catholic Institute for International Relations and Minority Rights Group); Lord Chitnis, *Free and Fair? The 1979 Rhodesian Election* (British Parliamentary Human Rights Group); Mick Delap, 'The April 1979 Elections in Zimbabwe-Rhodesia', 78 *African Affairs* (1979), 431–8; K. N. Mafuka, 'Rhodesia's Internal Settlement: a tragedy', 78 *African Affairs* (1979), 448–50; Miles Hudson, 'The Rhodesian Elections: a basis for the future', 35 *World Today* (1979), 324–32.

Zimbabwe's Southern African Setting[1]

by

James Barber

Open University

While it was the elegance of Lancaster House that provided the immediate physical setting for the 1979 Zimbabwe Conference, the conference's political setting was a broad international one—involving many more participants than those seated round the negotiating table. Indeed some of the delegates inside Lancaster House might have been excused had they sat with their heads half turned, straining to catch the advice, admonition, or support of those outside. These 'outsiders' ranged from the London-based officials of states and organisations to fleeting visitors like President Kaunda of Zambia or Mr Pik Botha from South Africa, and, in the case of the British ministers, attention had to be given to the noises off from Washington and from their own party.

The foundation of the Lancaster House Conference had been laid internationally—at the Commonwealth Conference in Lusaka in August 1979. There Mrs Thatcher and Lord Carrington had surprised their critics, and perhaps even themselves, by recruiting the support of the whole Commonwealth for a new British initiative. Before the conference there had been dire warnings of the opposition that Mrs Thatcher would face, especially as she was known to favour the constitutional arrangements and the election that had brought Bishop Abel Muzorewa into power. Had she faced such hostility it would have been no new experience for a British Prime Minister at a Commonwealth Conference. Ever since UDI Britain has been in the Commonwealth dock over Rhodesia, but now by a combination of skilled diplomacy, a determination to gain a settlement, and the fortune of favourable circumstances, Mrs Thatcher had been able to turn the tables. The importance of this shift in the Commonwealth's stance cannot be over-emphasised. Instead of Britain finding herself alone, or at best supported by the old White dominions, she was now working with her severest critics, the Black states, and some of these states were those on whom the Patriotic Front relied for its support.

The Lusaka background to the conference underlines the international dimension to Zimbabwe's recent history. One aspect of that has been the global setting, illustrated by the United Nations sanctions against the old

White regime, but here the concentration is on the Southern African setting. Although the cruel war which has ravaged Zimbabwe is a 'civil war' (for ultimately it is concerned with who exercises power there) it has involved the whole sub-continent. Nor will the neighbouring states escape the consequences of the new Zimbabwe political order, whatever that may be. UDI and the war dragged all her neighbours into Zimbabwe's affairs—without, for instance, the support of South Africa (and originally Portugal) the Smith regime could not have survived as it did, and without the support of the Front Line states the Patriotic Front could not have waged its guerilla campaign.

Although by 1979 the principal parties to the Zimbabwe war (i.e. the Muzorewa Government and the two wings of the Patriotic Front) were weary of the conflict, their anxiety for peace was not such that they were prepared to accept any settlement. The situation inside Zimbabwe was far from clear cut. Despite the success of the Patriotic Front in mounting a guerilla war that had forced the Whites to accept Black majority rule, the immediate political fruits had fallen to Muzorewa whom the Patriotic Front regarded as a puppet of the Whites. The situation was equally unsatisfactory for Muzorewa, however, as he had been unable to fulfil his promise to end the war or gain international recognition. On the military front there was stalemate, with the government forces unable to rid the country of the guerillas, while on their side the guerillas, for all the disorder they had created, were unable to inflict a final defeat on the government. In their own distinctive ways the forces of the government and the Patriotic Front were still in the field and fully capable of fighting on, but neither had the prospect of a quick victory.

As they had not achieved their objectives, and as, with continued external support, they were capable of continued fighting, it seems doubtful if left to their own devices Robert Mugabe and Joshua Nkomo of the Patriotic Front, or Muzorewa and his supporters would have been prepared to negotiate a settlement in 1979. It was their dependence on external support that explains why, despite the continued bitterness between them, and despite the absence of a clear military victory, the parties agreed to attend the conference, and why, once they were there, they conceded point after point to the British position. The dependence that Smith had had to place on South Africa to survive had been inherited by Muzorewa. He was no less reliant than the White government had been on the Republic's economic support and for the materials (and even men) to wage the war. The South African Government was eager for a settlement to the long Zimbabwe crisis, and they had shown during Smith's period in power that they were not afraid to exert pressure to try to gain it. Smith had often resented this, as in 1975 when he complained that South African interference resulting in the abortive Victoria Falls Conference had ruined his chance of reaching an agreement with Muzorewa, and that South Africa's attempts at detente in Africa generally were undermining the White position in Rhodesia.[2] Yet in the following year, after Kissinger's shuttle diplomacy, he was forced again by South Africa not only to reopen negotiations—this time in Geneva—but to accept for the first time the principle of Black majority rule.

On their part the Patriotic Front's guerilla armies were dependent on the Black Front Line states for their bases, training facilities, and for affording them international legitimacy. Added to these they depended on communist states for military supplies and training.

The Black Front Line states had bitterly opposed UDI from the beginning. They saw it not only as illegal and as a source of instability on their borders, but a racist act. When sanctions failed to bring down the Smith regime—as the black states had predicted—they had been prepared to support and harbour the guerilla armies. But after years of involvement, and the partial victory of removing Smith's government, the Front Line states became increasingly reluctant to support indefinitely a costly, bloody war. In the first place they had serious economic problems, which were partly caused by the war, and which certainly could not be resolved until it was ended. This was true even of Tanzania, which although not bordering on Zimbabwe had in overthrowing Idi Amin in Uganda exacerbated her own economic problems. For the states which did border Zimbabwe, notably Zambia and Mozambique, there were even more substantial problems. The guerilla armies, which they housed, and which were not always well disciplined, had created internal security problems, and they had proved a further drain on the economy. Even more serious were the raids by Rhodesian forces to attack guerilla bases and the country's supply system. The situation in Zambia became particularly bleak. With increasing economic and communications problems (not all of which were created by the war) the Zambians were forced to rely again on their southern neighbours, including the very people against whom the guerilla armies were fighting. (Ironically Joshua Nkomo's guerilla forces probably lived off imported Zimbabwe maize at the time of the Conference.) Therefore, despite the personal commitment of leaders like Presidents Kaunda of Zambia and Machel of Mozambique to the cause of the Patriotic Front, these same leaders showed increasing anxiety to end the ruinous war.

Mrs Thatcher and Lord Carrington were fortunate that their initiative at Lusaka coincided with this war weariness. This in no way detracts from their diplomatic skill and determination, for even with these more favourable circumstances reaching a settlement was no easy task. Without this coincidence of interests, however, no degree of diplomatic skill could have succeeded.

*   *   *   *   *   *

This paper has been completed immediately after the Lancaster House conference, before the terms of the agreement have been implemented. The chronic uncertainty about Zimbabwe's future persists. Looking to that future the agreement has changed the international situation enabling Britain to jettison her formal responsibility for Zimbabwe, but has it changed anything else? Was the coincidence of interests that made the agreement possible only temporary, leaving the potential for conflict as great as ever? The answers to these questions lie partly in Zimbabwe itself and partly in developments across Southern Africa with constant interaction between the two. In both cases a tension exists between aspirations which in the normal courses of events would lead to greater cooperation and those which lead to continuing conflict. This tension between the forces of cooperation and conflict will shape the relationships within Southern Africa over the next decade.

Within Zimbabwe rapid recovery from the war (whether in economic, social, or political terms) will require relative stability and a high degree of cooperation between the diverse groups. Whoever holds political power, and whatever their ideology, they are likely to call for that stability and cooperation. The message from the government will be to put the bitterness of the past behind and work in harmony to rebuild the country. However, there is also a clear potential for continued conflict. The leaders, groups, tribes, and armies which for years have contested for power will not lightly abandon their ambitions or forget their sacrifices. Even if Zimbabwe could be isolated from the rest of Southern Africa the internal tension between conflict and cooperation would be strong and difficult to manage. But Zimbabwe cannot be isolated from tensions which stretch across the sub-continent.

In Southern Africa as a whole the advantages of stability and cooperation are as clear as they are in Zimbabwe (although in this case it concerns relationships between states rather than groups within the states). Those who stress this cooperative approach could point first to the individual and social advantages of peace, of bringing an end to killing and destruction. Then they could note the degree of interdependence that has been found in the past and the advantages of building on this for the future. They could underline the common problems that are faced which can best be solved in partnership—the need to improve agricultural practices, to raise the standard of living of those at subsistence level, to extend education and training. They could also point to the great potential of the region, not least the mineral wealth, which can only be fully developed if there is peace and coordination of effort. By combining their efforts, by avoiding friction and concentrating on material wealth, all the peoples of Southern Africa could, according to this view, benefit from the riches that are around them. Part of the strength of this argument lies in the amount of cooperation that has existed and continues to exist. For instance the movement of people across state frontiers, with large numbers of unskilled workers moving onto the farms and into the factories and mines of South Africa and Rhodesia, and the no less important movement of small numbers of skilled men transporting their 'know how', e.g. crane drivers and technicians from South Africa who have recently moved into the port at Maputo in Mozambique to fill places vacated by the Portuguese). There are also shared marketing facilities, and in the case of South Africa and her three small neighbours—Botswana, Lesotho, and Swaziland—a customs union. There are joint scientific and research activities, and perhaps most noticeable of all, there are shared communication and transport facilities. No less than six Southern African states have no seaboard (Zambia, Zimbabwe, Malawi, Botswana, Lesotho, and Swaziland). To have contact with the outside world each of these states has to achieve some form of agreement with its neighbours, and to place reliance on them.

The general picture presented by this cooperative perception is of the states of the sub-continent, whatever their political ideologies, working together to achieve common goals, and cooperating in the movement of people, goods, capital, technology, and ideas. Taken to its extreme this image would present a functional ideal in which economic and technical priorities were dominant, and political divisions of little or no consequence. Yet, even if this extreme image is not accepted the states of Southern Africa do appreciate that their development priorities can only be achieved by interdependence, by achieving a working relationship with their neighbours.

The recognition of this interdependence is most strongly voiced in South Africa. In 1968 three South African economists—J. A. Lombard, J. J. Stadler, and P. J. van der Merwe, gave their version of it. They wrote of 'systematic co-operation', which was 'a clear alternative to *isolation* on the one hand, and *integration* on the other hand. The idea of systematic co-operation is to obtain the best of both worlds of politics and economics respectively, or perhaps more reasonably, to obtain the optimum combination of political independence and economic viability for the various culturally homogeneous population groups.' They argued for much greater economic integration in the sub-continent and in particular an increase in the flow of goods at the expense of labour. 'In short', they wrote, 'without necessarily reducing the R3,641 million trade with the rest of the world, the *percentage* dependence on the rest of the world could be reduced by rapidly increasing the inter-regional trade at present valued at about R651 million. *This would be the target.*'[3]

Similar arguments have been advanced by South Africans whenever they have advocated detente with their Black neighbours. Lief Egeland, a distinguished, retired South African diplomat addressing a meeting in Salisbury in November 1978, spoke of his hopes that 'the interdependence of the region's various economies on one another will prove to be a more durable influence in the long run on the overall direction of Southern Africa than the ephemeral political attitudes of today'. He dismissed the idea that South Africa was trying to practice economic imperialism, stressing that the countries of the region 'share a common economic destiny that has nothing to do with imperialism. . . The destiny we share is not some sort of neo-colonialism. Rather it is based on a common economic environment inhabited by us all and upon which we all depend for our existence.' He concluded by saying that while he realised that 'the growing factors of interdependence cannot be relied upon to shape or materially influence political or racial attitudes, they can induce a sense of heightened realism, and make for that reciprocal understanding to which I have referred'.[4] Egeland's statement brings out forcibly the main thrust of the White South African view—that common economic interests are more permanent and basic than the ephemeral political attitudes of the day, and that interdependence should introduce what they see as 'realism' into the situation.

With their powerful economy and eagerness to defuse political tensions

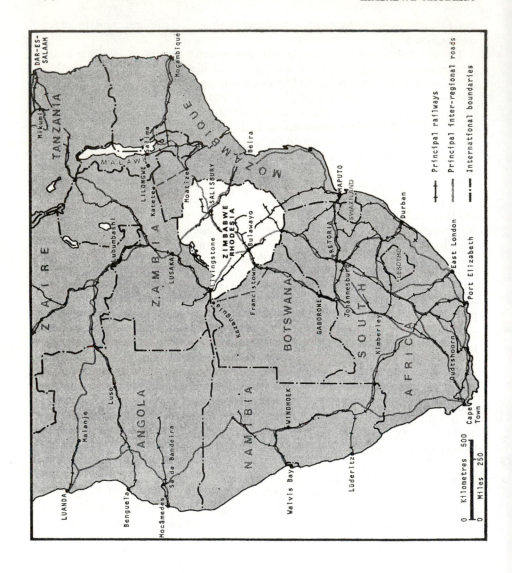

I am indebted to Mr John Hunt of the Open University for preparing this map

there are obvious advantages for the White South Africans in promoting regional interdependence, in emphasing economic priorities, and trying to depoliticise the situation. Yet the degree of interdependence in Southern Africa has also been underlined by the problems experienced by states which have attempted to break away from their regional ties. The most striking has been Zambia's efforts after Rhodesia's UDI. Before UDI Zambia, which is landlocked with no short route to the sea, relied upon the rail and road routes through Rhodesia as her main outlets. However, she has other options and it is these which she tried to develop to break her dependence on Rhodesia. The alternatives include links by road, and more recently by rail, to Dar es Salaam on the East coast, a route through Malawi using road and rail. a link with South Africa through Kazangula in Botswana which avoids Rhodesia, and the Benguela railway to the Angolan coast. None of these alternatives have been entirely satisfactory. The Rhodesians succeeded in closing the route through Kazangula, while that through Malawi has a very limited capacity. The Zambians placed great faith in the new rail link to Dar es Salaam, which was built with speed and efficiency by the Chinese, but, in the short term at least, it has not lived up to its expectations—it has suffered from inefficiency, and, because of problems at the port and with rolling stock, its carrying capacity has been less than anticipated. Instead of creating a bond between the Tanzanian and Zambian governments there is the danger that it will be a source of increasing friction. If the line to Dar es Salaam was less successful than anticipated the Benguela railway more than lived up to expectations during the mid-1970s. In 1973 and 1974 that route took roughly half Zambia's foreign trade by volume,[5] but then, as the internal war spread in Angola, the line was first disrupted and then closed. Although President Kaunda recognised the MPLA government of Angola in April 1974, having previously supported the rival UNITA party, that did not change the position, for the UNITA forces controlled part of the country through which the railway passed and were able to close the line. Following the closure Zambia was forced to reduce the export of copper—its critical export leader—and to limit its imports thereby causing severe shortages of equipment and goods. The Zambian economy, already in serious trouble from internal problems, faced a crisis. It was this perilous situation that forced President Kaunda to reopen again the southern route through Rhodesia in 1979 (as well as searching for additional international aid and putting pressure on the Patriotic Front to reach a settlement).

Despite the international sanctions directed against them the Rhodesians did not have the same difficulties. Their traditional outlets are through South Africa and Mozambique. Originally the line of rail to South Africa passed through Botswana, but a direct link has now been created over Beit Bridge. Since UDI the routes through Mozambique have been seriously disturbed, first by the British oil blockade of the port of Beira, but much more seriously following the overthrow of Portuguese rule. The Rhodesians overcame this problem by increasing their use of the South African outlet, although this served to underline more than ever their reliance on the Republic and the pressure that the South African government could exert.

The Zambian experience may be an extreme example of the problems of dependence in Southern Africa, but Zimbabwe is also landlocked and whatever the political complexion of her government she will have to keep open her external routes. The lesson for both Zimbabwe and Zambia is that to survive they are dependent upon others, and, while in terms of routes they each have more than one option, all outlets have some degree of unreliability and expose the landlocked state to pressure.

Nor are the constraints imposed by the interdependence of Southern Africa confined to the landlocked states. They are further illustrated when governments with opposing ideologies are forced to work together. This is the case with South Africa and independent Mozambique. President Machel's government has inherited a poor, weak economy, and a shortage of skilled manpower. To develop the country external trade and aid is required, and South Africa is in the best position to provide much of that. Hence the Mozambique authorities have kept open the port of Maputo for South African trade and have continued to send (although in smaller numbers) unskilled workers to the Republic. For their part South Africa has placed some reliance on Mozambique; although to describe it as 'dependence' would be setting it too high. The South Africans have continued to use Maputo as a port—with its dual advantages of providing the shortest route to the sea from the northern Transvaal and its specialised handling facilities for minerals—and to take the bulk of the power from the giant Cabora Bassa dam on the Zambesi in Mozambique.

The lesson is clear. None of the states of Southern Africa can escape from some form of involvement and reliance upon their neighbours, but the degree of reliance and the pattern of relationships is different in each case. As it is impossible to take a political stance without taking some account of the economic circumstances, so it is equally impossible to isolate economic and technological considerations from the political setting. That was clear even in the old colonial days, long before guerilla armies took to the field.

In the early 1950s when the British authorities were considering a federation in East Africa, which might possibly be linked to the Central Africa Federation, a survey was made for a possible rail route to draw the two great blocks of Africa together. Nothing came of that, but when the Central African Federation was established there were implications for the whole sub-continent, and a clear attempt by the British to draw their territories, and especially Rhodesia, out of the South African orbit. In South Africa a National Party Government, for whom the British had little warmth, was imposing its policy of *apartheid,* while the British were pursuing their ideal of multiracial government. Although the transport links with the south remained the dominant outlet of the Federation, the new political development was reflected in the changing pattern of trade. In the face of a protective barrier, South Africa's trade with the Federation declined while Rhodesia's position flourished. By the time the Federation was disbanded in 1964 Rhodesia had become the manufacturing centre of Central Africa, being the main supplier of goods to Zambia and Malawi.[6] After UDI that was changed, for the trade pattern again responded to the political developments. Rhodesian industry, cut off from its external markets, concentrated on supplying the beleagured home market, while her exports were mainly primary products, especially minerals and agricultural produce. Meanwhile, and somewhat ironically, South Africa regained some of her market for manufactured goods.

The British attempt of colonial days to draw the Central Africa Federation away from South Africa's embrace was a political decision which ran against the economic grain. Yet it is the type of action that must tempt all South Africa's neighbours. The South African economy is a giant among pygmies. This is clear from the following table of economic indicators which shows how the South African economy is built on a different scale to those of its neighbours. There is such an imbalance of economic power in the subcontinent that it has political consequences. If that was a matter of concern for the White colonial powers, it is clearly even more so for the independent Black states. No independent state relishes economic domination by a neighbour, and will try to break or modify that dominance. Even a small state like Lesotho, which is completely surrounded by South Africa, has demonstrated that limited options are open for her. While her economic dependence on the Republic remains—including a large movement of Lesotho men to work in South Africa—politically and diplomatically the Lesotho government has kept its powerful neighbour at a distance, criticised her at the OAU and the UN, and has gained aid from a variety of donors.[7]

Southern Africa—Economic Indicators

	Gross National Product (Market Prices 1976)	Per Capita Income 1977 ($)	Trade 1977	
			Imports	Exports
	($ billions)		($ millions)	($ million)
Angola	1.8	300	340	500
Botswana	0.3	390	197	161
Lesotho	0.3	240	—	—
Malawi	0.7	140	235	195
Mozambique	1.4	150	283	220
Namibia	0.9	—	350	615
South Africa	33.7	1,340	5,893	6,158
Swaziland	0.3	540	197	165
Zaire	3.2	130	610	981
Zambia	2.3	450	828	897
Zimbabwe	3.5	500	—	—

Source: 1978 World Bank Atlas and 1978 and 1979 World Development Report by the World Bank. I am indebted to Michael Spicer for obtaining these figures.

A recent attempt to modify or even break South Africa's hold was initiated in July 1979, when the five Black Front Line states (Tanzania, Zambia, Botswana, Angola, and Mozambique) called a conference at Arusha to which they invited the representatives of Western states, international organisations, and banks. Clearly there was a strong political motive behind the meeting, as Sir Seretse Khama made clear at the beginning when he stated that because many Black states were forced to rely on South Africa while condemning her evil policies, the aim was to change the economic and transport dependence. In their final communique the leaders recognised that they had only taken a first step, and hoped that in the future they would be joined by 'free' Zimbabwe and Namibia. Recognising that their aims were essentially long term they decided to give first priority to reorientating the transport and communications system, and established a transport and communications commission. They also decided to call a further and larger meeting with potential donors. The donors who had attended the first meeting gave a sympathetic hearing, but no undertakings. They noted the large scale of the proposed development—an estimated £700 billion to reorganise the region's communications away from South Africa.

Although Zimbabwe was not represented at the Arusha meeting, she also will try to extend her future options. Plainly she will have to continue to place heavy reliance on South Africa, but the degree to which this is regarded as tolerable and the energy she exerts to try to break away will be determined by political developments. In economic terms Zimbabwe is second only to South Africa in the sub-continent (although far behind the Republic). If Zimbabwe can recover from the ravages of war—and again this may well rest on the political dispensation inside the country and in the sub-continent—the strength of her economy will create opportunities to develop links not only with her neighbours but outside Southern Africa in a way that is not open to the weaker economies. Potential options are therefore available, but these cannot remove the reliance that she must continue to place on neighbours, not least because of her land locked position.

Despite her relative economic strength and despite the options that this opens up for her, Zimbabwe, like all Southern African states, will continue to feel the weight of South Africa's great economic power. If, however, the main strain on relationships in Southern Africa were this imbalance created by South Africa's economic strength, it could be managed within the context of the sub-continent. But that is not the case. Southern Africa is an arena for two major international conflicts. The first concerns race. The Black states feel this particularly strongly, for, as Julius Nyerere said, the freedom they have sought is 'without distinction of race, colour or religion. Racialist minority governments cannot be acknowledged because they are a negation of our very existence. Co-existence is impossible; for if the African peoples of South Africa and Rhodesia have no human rights to govern themselves, then what is the basis of Tanzania's existence, of Zambia's, of Kenya's, and so on?'[8] For Black leaders the struggle in Southern Africa is seen as a chapter of the fight against colonialism, and for some even against slavery. In his 1979 Reith lectures Professor Ali Mazrui stated that:

the system in South Africa is an amalgam of slavery and colonisation. Apartheid shares with slavery the assumption of hereditary caste roles, status-based partly on descent and partly on ascriptive rule of master and servant. Just as racism and contempt for the black people were at the core of the slave trade, so once again are racism and contempt for black people at the core of apartheid.[9]

The Black nationalist struggle against White rule in Southern Africa has developed over the post-war years from political agitation against British colonial rule, through the long wars against Portugal, to the conflict in Zimbabwe. In South Africa itself African nationalism (mainly but not exclusively represented by the African National Congress (ANC)) has passed through three distinct phases—first an elite reformist period, second, a broader based revolutionary but non-violent time, and finally a violent revolutionary phase.[10] If the struggle for South Africa develops as the Black nationalists predict, the whole sub-continent will be consumed, so that in retrospect the conflict in Zimbabwe may appear only as a prologue to a larger, fiercer war.

The anti-imperialist drive, which is now directed against the White rulers of South Africa, and Black 'puppets'—like Muzorewa and the rulers of the Black homelands in South Africa—has achieved a broad international dimension because of the success of the Black states in legitimising their cause through international organisations, and linking it to the call for a new international order. In Southern Africa this implies overthrowing White minority rule, to rebuild a new and more just society. The international dimension of the claims were made clear in a broadcast to South Africa in January 1975 from the ANC's Radio Freedom in Zambia. 'In the final analysis' it was stated, 'the issue between us and our rulers in South Africa is an international issue.' A distinction was drawn between those who believe in justice and sharing the world's wealth, and 'those who believe in injustice and in exploitation of man by man and the domination of nations by others . . . in the exploitation of the many by the few, in short, in inhumanity and injustice'. The voice of the ANC had no doubt of the outcome. 'The world which supports our cause is a growing one while the world which South Africa represents is fact diminishing . . . there is a tide of revolutionary change which is sweeping across the face of the globe'.[11]

Such confidence in the final outcome is partly based on the success of the Black nationalist armies in overthrowing White rule in the Portuguese territories and in Rhodesia, but it is also based on the view of some Black nationalist leaders (and it should be stressed that it is only 'some') that they are in the vanguard of a struggle in which the international class structure based on imperialism is inevitably being overthrown. As the Marxist states have become the main suppliers of the materials to wage war, so a form of neo-Marxism has become increasingly important as the intellectual framework by which some Black nationalist leaders explain the world, and as a motivator for their actions. From this viewpoint race and class are merged together in a great international struggle, and the Black peoples of Southern Africa are united in a revolutionary cause. Oliver Tambo, the ANC President General, told a London audience in 1973 that 'Southern Africa is becoming the new battleground in the conflict between the oppressed and the oppressor, and. . . all our enemies are pinned together in an international colonialist conspiracy whose aim is to maintain the status quo in our region'. He said that the liberation movements were 'objectively required to recognise the mutual interdependence of our struggles in South Africa, Nambia, Mozambique, Zimbabwe, Angola, Guinea Bissau and other parts of Africa.

This mutual interdependence equally derives from our historic responsibilities to complete . . . the liberation of the African continent.'[12]

That view of the sources of conflict links directly with the second way in which Southern Africa is seen as an arena for a major international struggle. This is the conflict between East and West. While the neo-Marxists see a racial-cum-class conflict in terms of a structured relationship based on capitalist exploitation, this second approach sees Southern Africa as part of the struggle between communism and the 'free world'. Those who hold this 'power politics' view would dismiss the claims of the black revolutionaries that they are seeking justice and equality as so much hypocrisy. The revolutionaries are not, so this argument is put, interested in achieving such liberal ideas but rather in imposing Marxist dictatorships. They are not seeking freedom, they are seeking totalitarian power. In doing this movements like the ANC and the Patriotic Front become instruments of the communist states whose aim is to extend their sphere of control and strangle the 'free world'. As support for their views the advocates of this 'power politics' approach point to the backing the communist states have given to the revolutionary movements in Southern Africa—ANC, PF, MPLA, etc.—and to the avowed Marxist commitment of many of the leaders of these movements. They also point to the involvement of communist states, like East Germany, in the training of security forces in some Black states, and, even more to the Cuban military involvement in Angola, which, seen from this perspective, is a direct communist conquest of the territory—an extension of Marxist imperialism.

The strongest advocates of this perspective are the Whites of Southern Africa, who believe that they are the upholders of Western values and interests, although usually unrecognised as such, even in the West. The White South Africans are not, however, entirely alone in this viewpoint. They have always had support from 'right wing' elements in the West, and more recently Western concern has grown with the realisation of the degree of dependence on Southern Africa for minerals, and fears that the Cuban involvement does represent an extension of the East/West conflict into the sub-continent. It was such concern and fears that prompted Henry Kissinger's attempts in 1976 to settle Southern African problems so that the region would not become increasingly embroiled in East/West conflict, and itself provide a new source of tension. While Kissinger's initiative failed and the new US administration of President Carter adopted a different stance toward the sub-continent, paying much greater respect to the ideal of human rights, Western fears persist about communist expansion. Moreover, there are Black leaders in Southern Africa who share some of these fears and oppose the ideology and methods of the revolutionaries. In Zimbabwe Abel Muzorewa and Robert Mugabe are not divided by different attitudes towards racial discrimination, for they both detest it. Nor can their rivalry be explained solely by their competing ambitions to lead the country, although that certainly comes into it, but by their differing ideologies and the methods they favour to bring change. Mugabe is a Marxist; Muzorewa is not. Mugabe believes in an armed struggle as the only way to power; Muzorewa believes in achieving change by less violent methods.

Although 'the power politics' perspective of the Southern African conflict is not confined to the Whites, they are certainly its loudest advocates and often give it an interpretation in which they play a dramatic leading role. In the past there was no stronger advocate of this than Ian Smith, who saw the Whites of Rhodesia upholding the cause of Western Christian civilisation against all the odds. The declaration of UDI was framed in these terms, and although he has now lost power Smith has not changed his views. Many South African Whites share Smith's views that communism has spread throughout Africa because colonial powers, like Britain, were not prepared to stand and fight for Western interests against the revolutionaries. Instead the Whites of Southern Africa have been deserted but that does not imply that they will not be prepared to fight—as they have already demonstrated in Zimbabwe—and in doing so they fight not only for themselves but for the West in general. In the words of the Unilateral Declaration of Independence having 'been prepared to shed their blood and give of their substance in what they believed to be a mutual interest of freedom-loving people, [the Rhodesians] now see all that they have cherished about to be shattered on the rocks of expediency'. Furthermore they 'have witnessed a process which is destructive of these very precepts upon which civilisation in a primitive country has been built, they have seen the principles of Western democracy and responsible government, and moral standards crumble elsewhere, nevertheless they have remained steadfast'.[13]

The mantle of remaining steadfast, of continuing the fight, has now fallen on the Whites of South Africa. As self-professed defenders of the West, and yet unrecognised as such in the West, White South Africans have identity problems. Ideally they would like to be embraced in the Western fold, and in the past had hopes that they could act as a bridge between the West and Black Africa, and/or be accepted into a relationship with the NATO alliance. Despite regular rebuffs, and the realisation now that the West will never agree to a formal alliance, traces of the old hopes persist. In June 1978, for instance, John Vorster appealed to the USA and Britain to cooperate with those who seek peace in Southern Africa, and, for the sake of the West in general, to 'make sure that South Africa does not fall prey to the Marxist onslaught'.[14] In September of that year P. W. Botha said that 'we must rely on the West and the free world, in whose defence we stand, to grant us a rightful place in the galaxy of nations'.[15] Yet while such hopes continued to be nurtured, frustration at the West's rejection was often more obvious. The West was frequently portrayed as weak and vacillating, unable or unwilling to defend its own interests against Third World and communist pressures. In October 1976 P. W. Botha (showing much less warmth than in the quotation above) said he had little faith in the 'timorous Western world which is so captivated by the soft music of detente from Moscow'.[16] In April 1978 he dismissed the idea that the West based its policy towards South Africa on morality for 'their consciences are soaked in the oil barrels of Nigeria'.[17] In its periods of greatest disillusionment the South African Government has rejected its own self-image by claiming to disassociate itself from the West. The latest demonstration of this came in March 1979 when Pik Botha, the Foreign Minister, announced that South Africa was taking a neutral stance between East and West. Characteristically, however, he associated this with a fresh attempt to establish closer relations with Black Africa. In its search for an international identity South Africa has swung regularly from an emphasis on being Western to one on being African. Yet it has failed to find easy acceptance as either. The latest African initiative became flesh in P. W. Botha's attempts to promote a 'constellation of states' in Southern Africa. This has close similarities to attempts by previous governments to establish detente with the Black states or implement an 'outward policy'. To achieve this predominantly African identity, the South Africans would have to quell the Black states' fears of economic exploitation, their repugnance at the Republic's racial policies, and their hesitation in accepting a regional framework in which South Africa would be dominant.

In advancing its views on the future of the sub-continent the South African Government emphasises the economic and technical advantages of cooperation, but these carry political implications. The South Africans want a sub-continent of separate states, each pursuing its national interest (interpreted not in broad ideological terms, but in terms of economic development), each respecting the sovereign rights of others (including non-interference in domestic affairs), and each refusing to harbour guerillas. Inevitably South Africa wants to retain and even extend its powerful position, so that neighbouring states in cooperation with and to some extent dependent on her, will have a stake in a stable and powerful Republic. In contrast the ANC believe that cooperation in Southern Africa can only flourish after a successful revolution in the Republic. Then a 'free' South Africa will be able to help her neighbours, working together not only from common economic interests, but from a shared revolutionary experience. This merging of liberated peoples will be led by the revolutionary parties which have been in the vanguard of the struggle and have learned to work together and to establish a common ideology in adversity.[18]

In summary therefore there are two broad perspectives in which Southern Africa is seen as an arena for continuing international conflict. First as part of a racial (cum class) struggle, and second as part of the contest between East and West. Whether these perspectives are seen separately or overlapping each other, they provide a sharp contrast with the approach which emphasises the need for cooperation and stability and the importance of interdependence.

*   *   *   *   *

Assessing the prospects for the next decade, the most critical unknown is whether open warefare will continue within Zimbabwe and/or Southern Africa generally. It seems unlikely that the situation will be absolutely clear cut, with either all-out war or virtually complete peace. The tension between conflict and cooperation will persist, producing a degree of instability and violence.

The war in Zimbabwe may continue despite the Lancaster House agreement and the new elections. The parties to the conflict could remain virtually the same, but alternatively there could be splits and new groupings, even among those who previously fought together, including the possibilities that tribal divisions could become more overt, or the military leaders who have been in the field could play a more prominent political role. If the fighting does continue the neighbouring states, despite their anxiety to see an end to the conflict, will not be able to avoid a continuing involvement. There is the further possibility that, with formal British responsibility removed, the degree of international involvement may intensify and change in kind. If the South Africans continued to back one of the parties while the Black Front Line states backed another, the perception of Zimbabwe as a cockpit for a racial-cum-class struggle would be stronger than ever. No longer would the cloak of a united international effort to return Zimbabwe to legality under the British be available. There was international agreement on this, and economic sanctions were a demonstration of the international community acting in harmony to achieve that end. This may have helped to channel away some attention of the 'super powers', and their proxies. There is a danger, therefore, that if the war continues in Zimbabwe its international dimensions will become wider and more serious than before.

Even if relative stability could be achieved inside Zimbabwe, the new state faces the further danger of involvement in the power struggle for South Africa itself. If that struggle does develop into war the Zimbabwe government may try to stand aside, but, with conflict all around her and the passions and sacrifices of her own recent history so fresh in the mind, it would be a difficult and lonely furrow to plough. Moreover whatever the attitude of the Zimbabwe government, a South African war would seriously and adversely affect the Zimbabwe economy. The alternative of backing one of the sides is no more enticing. If she were to support the Black guerilla forces similar problems would arise to those which have haunted Zambia— of a new state trying to create national unity and develop the economy while there is war on her borders, guerilla armies on her soil, regular heavy raids from the opposing government forces, and major disruption of the the transport and communications system. Also like Zambia it is likely that some reliance would have to be placed on South Africa, however opposed the Zimbabwe government might feel to her values and policies. If, on the other hand, a Zimbabwe government came into power which was prepared to support the South Africans, there is the real danger of becoming an occupied country and having South Africa's war fought on her soil; together with the problems of housing an alien army. The potential scale and bitterness of a South African war between the South African Government and the Black guerilla armies (with external support for both sides) is so great that the whole of Southern Africa could be torn apart. The armies would make a desert and the victors call it peace.

The chances of obtaining relative peace and stability either in Zimbabwe or more generally in Southern Africa look far from certain. It seems unlikely that South Africa's Black neighbours will adopt the attitude of unquestioning cooperation which is assumed in P. W. Botha's proposals for a constellation of states. However, while continuing to condemn the Republic's racial policies the neighbouring states may decide that however good the cause the price of violent confrontation is too high. Yet this approach rests on the doubtful assumptions that substantial conflict will not develop within South Africa itself, drawing in the surrounding territories, and that the Black states will not be prepared to pay the price of some form of armed confrontation. The final possibility is that there would be such rapid and substantial reform in South Africa that the governments of the Black states and many Blacks inside the Republic—if not the revolutionary parties' armies in the field—would be satisfied with the progress being made and cooperate with a reformed South African Government.

For Zimbabwe the next decade will be shaped by the tension within her own borders and across Southern Africa between those aspirations which can only be achieved by cooperation and those which can be achieved by force.[19]

NOTES

1. For simplicity I have mainly used the name 'Zimbabwe', but when referring to specific past events or attitudes I have used 'Rhodesia'.
2. *Guardian,* 14 October 1975.
3. *The Concept of Economic Co-operation in Southern Africa* (Pretoria, 1968), 9 and 34.
4. Lief Egeland, *Interdependence in Southern Africa* (South African Institute of International Affairs, Johannesburg, 1978), 4.
5. Julian Burgess, *Interdependence in Southern Africa* (Economist Intelligence Unit, Special Report No 32, London, 1976), 44. The figures for 1973 were: Lobito 51.2 per cent, Dar es Salaam 26.9 per cent, Mombasa 6.8 per cent, Malawi 9 per cent, others 4.1 per cent.
6. *Ibid.,* 23.
7. David Hirschmann, 'Changes in Lesotho's Policy Towards South Africa, 78 *African Affairs* (April 1979).
8. Julius Nyerere, *Freedom and Socialism* (London, 1968), 374.
9. Ali Mazui 'The Cross of Humiliation', *Listener,* 15 November 1979, 658.
10. Leonard Thompson, *Politics in the Republic of South Africa* (Boston, 1966,) 165.
11. *ANC Speaks: Documents and Statements of the African National Congress 1955–1976,* 154.
12. *Ibid.,* 148.
13. Text of UDI in Donald Smith, *Rhodesia the Problem* (London, 1969), Appendix D, 117.
14. Quoted by Dean Geldenhuys, *The Neutral Option and Sub-Continental Solidarity* (South African Institute of International Affairs, Johannesburg, 1979), 5.
15. *Ibid.,* 5.
16. *Ibid.,* 4.
17. *Ibid.,* 5.
18. This view was put to me by an ANC representative in Lusaka.
19. Other articles dealing with relationships in Southern Africa include Larry Bowman, 'The Subordinate State System of Southern Africa', 12 *International Studies Quarterly* (1968), and Kenneth W. Grundy, 'Economic Patterns in the New Southern African Balance' in Gwendolen M. Carter and Patrick O'Meara (eds), *Southern Africa:The Continuing Crisis* (London, 1979).

The Insignificance of Tribe in the African Politics of Zimbabwe Rhodesia[1]

by

John Day

University of Leicester

I

The political divisions among Africans in Zimbabwe Rhodesia are bewilderingly complex. In 1979 one strained alliance of ZAPU (Zimbabwe African People's Union) and Robert Mugabe's ZANU (Zimbabwe African National Union) in the Patriotic Front confronted another strained alliance of UANC (United African National Council) and Ndabaningi Sithole's ZANU in the Government, while the new parties of ZDP (Zimbabwe Democractic Party) and NFZ (National Front of Zimbabwe) formed out of dissatisfaction with the old. This present complexity is not exceptional, for the antagonisms between and within the African parties of Zimbabwe Rhodesia have over the last twenty years been kaleidoscopic, as one pattern of fragmentation has succeeded another. This has resulted in curious paradoxes: for example, Mugabe, who helped Sithole in 1963 to establish ZANU in opposition to Joshua Nkomo's ZAPU, worked in 1979 with Nkomo against Sithole, while both Mugabe and Sithole claimed the inheritance of the original ZANU.

To help explain the apparently inexplicable many observers have assumed that tribal rivalries underlie many of the political differences between Africans in Zimbabwe Rhodesia. Often bitter quarrels have seemed improbably to be the consequences of trivial disagreements. Then it is tempting to look for weighty motives as the causes of serious political divisions. In the absence of any satisfactory explanation in terms of ideology, ultimate aim, basic strategy, or class, reference to supposed tribal animosities appears to give a substantial explanation, which is rooted in historical, geographical, and social realities. Unfortunately people often use tribe to explain African politics in Zimbabwe Rhodesia without providing adequate evidence or any aid to understanding precisely what tribe may mean in the Zimbabwe Rhodesian setting.

The Rhodesian Front Government, which represented the majority of the white settlers between 1962 and 1978, had an ideological vested interest in emphasising the tribal in African politics. It wished to believe that African nationalism, with its emphasis on the single African nation and on universal franchise, was in conflict with the traditional, tribal values that most Africans were supposed still to hold. In a document that it published in 1964 the Government quoted a memorandum prepared by the Ministry of Internal Affairs:

> Powerful African voices and deep sentiments are beginning to be aroused as they see their tribal values thrown into the melting pot or trodden on by a voting mass of literate youngsters herded together by a political boss.[2]

The Government argued against a referendum among Africans to test opinion on whether Rhodesia should be granted independence under the existing Constitution on the grounds that individuals voting would not represent the communal identities of the tribes. Wishing to believe that the Africans were unready to participate in modern government, the Rhodesian Front liked to stress the continuing tribal nature of African society and consequently emphasised the distinction between the two main tribal groups, the Shona and the Ndebele. The 1969 Constitution, for example, provided for four chiefs to represent the Shona and four to represent the Ndebele (a curious division, as the Ndebele formed only 22 per cent of the African population). Many Rhodesian whites believed that the Africans, even if they had a veneer of European civilisation, were still fundamentally primitive and feared that, without European control, they might revert to their traditional barbarism, which, in the European myth, entailed permanent and ubiquitous tribal wars. It was natural, then, to interpret antagonisms between African nationalists as the result of ingrained tribalism.

Eagerness to explain African politics in tribal terms is, however, by no means restricted to the Rhodesian right. To many journalists it is an instinctive reflex. In its most extreme form this preoccupation with tribe produces exaggerated statements like Smith Hempstone's that 'the tribe remains the most important element in black politics in Rhodesia',[3] and extravagant speculations like Paul Moorcraft's that 'Nkomo could perhaps seize Bulawayo, the traditional Ndebele capital, and set up a rival Ndebele state' to compete against a Shona republic based in Salisbury.[4] Less sweeping but still inadequately examined assumptions about tribe are common in the British press. A leading article in *The Guardian* in December 1977, for example, referred without scepticism to 'the fierce contest . . . between Matabele and Mashona which is widely feared'.[5] A report in *The Daily Telegraph* on the formation of NFZ appeared under the totally misleading headline, 'New party is ready for tribal poll in Rhodesia' and emphasised the party's Karanga rationale, in spite of its President's acknowledged statements that the party would not be solely for Karanga and that it had national policies.[6]

Excellent academic writers on Zimbabwe Rhodesia, too, often take tribe to be a crucial factor in African politics without much scrutiny. Larry W. Bowman asserted that, when the African National Congress was formed in 1957, 'the leadership was ethnically balanced',[7] assuming that the tribal mixture had some significance, whereas the composition of the

National Executive almost certainly resulted from the desire to represent fairly the two organisations, the Youth League, based in Salisbury, and the Bulawayo branch of the old Congress, whose merging had created the new Congress. Claire Palley, writing before the election of April 1979, talked as if it were axiomatic of 'the deep tribal divisions between the Shona and the Ndebele'.[8] Later, analysing the election results, she jumped hastily to the conclusion that the approximately 40 per cent of the total potential vote that Bishop Abel Muzorewa won correlated remarkably with the 43 per cent of the African population that belong to the Manyika, Korekore, and Zezuru tribes.[9] Yet the voting figures do not, in fact, show that Muzorewa received his support exclusively from these tribal areas.[10]

In some parts of Africa, like Nigeria and Kenya, tribal rivalry *has* been a major factor in modern politics, but one is not entitled to assume that this is true throughout the continent. The example of Zambia provides a salutary lesson. Robert Molteno has convincingly demonstrated that what may appear to be tribal conflicts are more accurately described as sectional.[11] His main thesis is well expressed in the passage he quotes from T. Rasmussen:

> ... the root causes of political competition [in Zambia] often lie in divergent economic and political interests, not in tribal differences... While tribe remains an important category of political analysis, it can be more usefully viewed as an aggregation of shared material interests rather than as an expression of traditional solidarity based on shared culture and historical experience and an innate hostility towards outsiders.[12]

In Zambia since independence political conflict has often been between *regions* competing for resources and offices that were in the government's gift. Zimbabwe Rhodesia provides no exact parallel, but the case of Zambia illustrates the danger of facile assumptions about tribal influence.

In this essay the thesis is advanced that tribe has not frequently been a major factor in the African politics of Zimbabwe Rhodesia and that, where it has intruded, it is difficult to give an intelligible explanation of why and how tribe has affected political behaviour. To forward this argument the next section tries to show that the ramifications of political development within the African nationalist movement can be explained more convincingly by dissatisfaction with leaders, rivalries for power, and differences of strategy than by tribe. Then follows an examination of the strongest cases that can be made for the impact of tribe on political activity, and the essay concludes with discussion of the difficulties raised by tribal explanations.

II

From its origins in the mid-1950s until 1961 the African nationalist movement in Southern Rhodesia achieved steadily increasing unity between various segments of the African population. To a degree that was unprecedented in the territory the African National Congress and, after it was banned in 1959, NDP (National Democratic Party) brought together in a single movement for African emancipation subsistence farmers and factory workers, the educated elite and the illiterate masses. Africans from the two principal cities, Salisbury and Bulawayo, cooperated in a way that had in the past proved impossible for more than a brief period. The nationalist leaders appealed successfully to Africans across nearly the whole country.

A constitutional conference in Salisbury in January to February 1961 marked a watershed in the history of the nationalist movement.[13] To win African representation at this conference was a major achievement for NDP, since the British and Southern Rhodesian governments had never previously recognised the Africans' right to a voice in constitutional development. At the same time the conduct of the NDP leaders under Nkomo at the conference led to serious disagreement within the Party, which, although largely stilled in 1961, re-emerged in 1963 to rend the movement in two and set the pattern in subsequent years of multiplying factionalism.

The cause of the crisis in the movement in 1961 was the agreement by Nkomo and his fellow delegates to a constitution in which Africans would for the first time have representatives in the Assembly, but initially with only fifteen seats out of sixty-five. The NDP delegation agreed reluctantly to this constitutional compromise, knowing that the Party had up to the conference demanded publicly one man, one vote, and that the National Executive had privately determined to accept nothing less than a constitution that would make NDP the main opposition in parliament. Widespread discontent with the constitutional agreement was immediately expressed within NDP and Nkomo very soon pretended that he had never accepted the compromise. Some in the party remained critical of Nkomo, who, nevertheless, skilfully managed to convince most members that he had not compromised NDP's principles. A few doubts about Nkomo's leadership lingered on and in June 1961 a splinter party, ZNP (Zimbabwe National Party), was formed by some malcontents. It attracted little support, but under the surface of general adulation of Nkomo ran a current of uncertainty that his handling of the constitutional conference had created.

In 1963 the movement split catastrophically when discontent with Nkomo's leadership led to revolt against him. The few who had since the conference been unhappy about Nkomo were joined by many more who had become increasingly disillusioned with him after the banning in September 1962 of ZAPU, the party which replaced NDP after its suppression in December 1961. When the Government outlawed ZAPU, Nkomo was out of the country and caused some concern by delaying his return, apparently in fear of what the authorities might do to him. As he had also been abroad in February 1959, when the Congress had been banned and its leaders arrested, and, as he had not returned home till November 1960, when recalled to be President of NDP, some people wondered if he lacked courage.

Although he did eventually go back to Southern Rhodesia and was restricted to the remote rural district where he was born, Nkomo again, and more seriously, raised doubts about his political judgement early in 1963. He persuaded the ZAPU Executive to leave the country for Dar es Salaam, although several of its members had doubts about the wisdom of leaving the people at home without leadership. These doubts were confirmed when the

ZAPU leaders found, contrary to what Nkomo had told them, that President Nyerere opposed their self-imposed exile. Some of Nkomo's lieutenants felt that his keenness to take them out of Southern Rhodesia formed part of a growing tendency in Nkomo to place his faith in an international strategy instead of confronting the government at home.[14] Throughout 1961 and 1962 Nkomo had personally spent much time in lobbying sympathisers around the world, an activity in which he had become skilled during his long exile after the banning of the Congress. Nkomo's purpose was to harden world opinion against the white minority regime in Southern Rhodesia, so that the British government would yield self-rule to the Africans. By 1963, however, this strategy had not achieved its objective.

Once people began to question Nkomo's political judgement, they could easily find other defects in his leadership. He had always left the organisation of the movement to others, and he lacked the ascetic intensity of Kaunda or Nyerere. Although he was an exciting orator to mass audiences, he was too easy-going in private to sustain confidence in his dynamism. His political skill seemed to lie more in his ability to rally the Party round his leadership than in directing the Party against its enemies.

Yet to some extent Nkomo became a scapegoat for some Africans' disappointment at the lack of progress that the nationalist movement had made towards majority rule, especially in comparison with the success of Africans in Northern Rhodesia and Nyasaland. The British Colonial Office gave way to pressure much more easily than the settler government of Southern Rhodesia. The rhetoric of the ZAPU leaders had raised hopes of early victory, but by 1963 the movement seemed to have reached an impasse. Secretly the Party leaders had begun to plan for violent resistance, but it was too early for tangible results.[15] Political frustration was released for some in denunciation of Nkomo.

By a curious irony Nkomo's tactic of leading his Executive into exile facilitated the organisation of opposition to him. As the ZAPU leaders dispersed round Africa, the dissidents did not challenge Nkomo in a full Executive meeting, which might have enabled him to re-assert his authority. In July 1963 a group of four ZAPU leaders meeting in Dar es Salaam tried to depose Nkomo as President and replace him with Sithole. The rebels knew that they had some popular support in Salisbury, but, ironically, in view of their criticism of Nkomo's preoccupation with activity abroad, they delayed their return home and allowed Nkomo to rally popular support there for his continuing leadership.[16]

Unable to prevent Nkomo from defending his position, Sithole and the other rebels formed a rival party, ZANU, in August 1963. Faced with this open challenge, Nkomo resurrected the banned ZAPU in the form of a nominally new organisation called PCC (People's Caretaker Council). The split in the nationalist movement became a developing disaster, as Africans lined up between the groups of rival leaders.

During the year in which the Government allowed the two nationalist parties legal existence PCC and ZANU became steadily more hostile to each other. The ideology and aims of the two factions were indistinguishable and, in spite of Sithole's criticism of Nkomo's strategy, ZANU in practice did

not immediately devise any radically new or more successful methods of
applying pressure on the government. Nkomo retained more popular support
than Sithole attracted, but ZANU recruited enough members to make it a far
more formidable opponent to PCC than ZNP, a mere splinter, had been to
NDP or ZAPU. The tragedy of the 1963 split was that both parties spent more
energy in denouncing each other than in fighting their common European
enemy. PCC and ZANU did not restrict their conflict to words and emotions:
many of their supporters used physical violence against each other. The
first year of ZANU's existence built up a legacy of bitterness and hatred
between the two nationalist groups which bedevilled many attempts in later
years to reconcile them.

When the Government banned PCC and ZANU in August 1964, it ended
one era for the nationalist movement and inaugurated another. Until then the
movement had grown in popularity and militancy, in spite of its division
and government repression. From 1964 to 1971 the movement went into a
period of paralysis in which the impetus gained in the previous years seemed
to have been lost. All the leaders of PCC, which still retained the name
ZAPU abroad, and ZANU were either arrested and held indefinitely without
trial or escaped to safety abroad. The government only slowly released
the nationalists from restriction or detention, the most senior, like Nkomo
and Sithole, remaining in confinement until 1974. Partly because the
experienced leaders were unavailable and partly because of the futility of
forming yet another party for the government to suppress, no mass party
was established in Rhodesia between 1964 and 1971. Those leaders who
set up headquarters in Zambia concentrated without marked success on
prosecuting guerilla war. In spite of efforts by the Organisation of African
Unity and individual African states to bring ZAPU and ZANU together,
they remained separate organisations in exile.

Far from re-uniting, both ZAPU and ZANU suffered internal divisions.
Early in 1970 a fierce quarrel broke out between the leaders of ZAPU,
which was never settled. Jason Moyo circulated a document criticising the
gross indiscipline of the guerilla army, the lack of cooperation between its
political and its military leaders, and the absence of strategic planning. He
also criticised the decision taken by James Chikerema, who was deputising
as leader while Nkomo was in captivity, to allow a British television company
to film the guerillas. Chikerema wrote an hysterical, almost megalomaniac,
reply, arguing that Nkomo had delegated power to him alone and that the
other political leaders who had helped form the ZAPU headquarters in
exile since 1964 had no independent authority. He asserted that they owed
their positions to him, that he had no obligation to consult them, and
announced his intention to take over the responsibilities previously delegated
to them. Moyo answered this by accusing Chikerema of precipitating a
crisis as serious as that created by the ZANU rebels in 1963, and by
rejecting Chikerema's claims to absolute authority over the Party.[17] In this
power struggle George Nyandoro supported Chikerema, while George
Silundika sided with Moyo. The guerillas divided their allegiance between
the rival groups of leaders and the conflict between the factions became
violent.

Eventually the ZAPU leaders, in spite of attempts by Kaunda and the Organisation of African Unity to bring them together, split irrevocably. The issue that, ironically, divided both ZAPU and ZANU, was whether the two parties should re-unite. Those leaders in both parties who wanted to heal the breach formed FROLIZI (Front for the Liberation of Zimbabwe) in October 1971. Chikerema and Nyandoro joined from ZAPU and a few officials below the highest rank from ZANU. Most of the senior figures in both parties refused to join FROLIZI, which consequently became merely a third, weaker nationalist party in exile.

A month later the British and Rhodesian Governments by agreeing on a constitution that failed to satisfy African aspirations unwittingly prompted the creation of an African political organisation that eventually provided an alternative focus of loyalty to the three nationalist parties in exile. For nine years Britain and Rhodesia had failed to find a constitution that was acceptable to both as the foundation of an independent Rhodesia, and in 1965 the Rhodesian Front had seized independence unilaterally. Eventually, in November 1971, the two Governments did reach agreement on an independence constitution, although Britain insisted that it could be implemented only if acceptable to the Rhodesian people as a whole. To ensure that the Africans said 'no' to the proposed constitution, some ZAPU and ZANU leaders who had been released from captivity established an organisation called ANC (African National Council). Bishop Muzorewa was persuaded to become the Chairman, because he had no association with either of the banned parties, ZAPU or ZANU. With him at the head of ANC and with the British Government insisting that there should be normal political activity while opinion on the constitution was being tested, the Rhodesian Government would find it hard to ban ANC. The new organisation performed successfully its chosen function of mobilising African opinion against the proposed constitution. The Commission under Lord Pearce that came out from Britain found the Africans overwhelmingly opposed to the settlement. In March 1972 ANC, having completed its original task, converted itself into a full political party with the traditional nationalist aim of one man, one vote. It differed from the three parties in exile only in method, as it sought its objectives through peaceful negotiation, not guerilla war. Muzorewa by temperament and belief was not disposed to violence and, more important, ANC would certainly have been banned if it had taken up arms against the Government.

At the end of 1974 another major development in the history of nationalism, the unification of the four parties by the Lusaka Agreement, was precipitated, like the formation of ANC, by events outside the movement. The initiatives that led to the Lusaka Agreement were taken by the Governments of South Africa and Zambia. Zambia had for long wanted an end to the illegal Rhodesian regime for ideological reasons and because the economic sanctions imposed on Rhodesia were also harming Zambia. South Africa by 1974 decided that it was in her interest to press the Rhodesian Prime Minister, Ian Smith, to hand over power to a moderate African government. Since the end of 1972 ZANU guerillas operating from Tete province in Mozambique, which was controlled by FRELIMO, sustained an unprecedentedly successful campaign in the north-east of Rhodesia, which strained the economic and military resources of the country. The situation threatened to become much more serious after the Lisbon coup of April 1974, because the new Portuguese policy of granting independence to Mozambique meant that ZANU guerillas would be able to move into Rhodesia along the whole of the 764 miles Mozambique frontier. South Africa was afraid that a rapidly expanding gueril'a war in Rhodesia and the eventual establishment of a militant guerilla regime in Salisbury would endanger its security. To prevent this South Africa used Rhodesia's economic dependence on South Africa to push Smith towards a settlement with the Africans. The Rhodesian Government agreed to release the nationalist leaders from detention.

Meanwhile the Zambian Government persuaded the four African parties to coalesce into one for the purpose of negotiating with the Rhodesian Front. Some of the officials from the militarily successful ZANU were reluctant to form a single organisation, although Zambia held out the incentive that the leaders who had spent over ten years in captivity would be freed to take part in normal political activity again. Eventually, in December 1974 ZAPU, ZANU, FROLIZI and ANC agreed to merge into a new ANC under the leadership of Muzorewa. Although he was the only African political leader who was then operating legally in Rhodesia and therefore the only one who was enjoying open popular support, Muzorewa was politically the least experienced and the least astute of the nationalist leaders. Many had regarded him as a caretaker leader while Nkomo and Sithole were imprisoned, but now he became the President of the first organisation since 1963 to embrace all African nationalists.

The newly formed unity was loose from the start, because of differences in attitude between the leaders of ANC about the guerilla war. All had agreed at Lusaka to try to negotiate a settlement with Ian Smith, but all declared that, if talking failed to achieve majority rule, ANC would use force to reach its objective. Nkomo, Sithole, and Chikerema were prepared to suspend guerilla war to test Smith's willingness to negotiate a satisfactory settlement, while Muzorewa was prepared for the first time openly to contemplate the necessity of a violent solution if talks failed. From the start of the new ANC Muzorewa was the most optimistic about the likelihood of a negotiated settlement, while Sithole was most pessimistic and Nkomo took an intermediary position. These attitudes seemed related to the strength of the guerilla army that each leader could hope to command: the old ANC had had no army, ZAPU's was weak, and ZANU's was formidable. Sithole's best hope of becoming the first leader of an independent Zimbabwe seemed to be if majority rule was won by ZANU arms. The ZANU guerilla commanders did not meticulously observe the ceasefire that had been agreed at Lusaka, as they were afraid of losing the advantage that they had won in the field. Sithole's militancy reflected that of the ZANU soldiers. His reputation as the most extreme of the ANC leaders was enhanced by the Government's treating him as the most dangerous and by his re-arrest in February 1975 (although he was soon released again).

These differences of attitude towards the guerilla war did not cause dissension between the leaders in ANC, but severe strain did develop over when a national congress should be held to elect an executive. This was crucial because the elections might significantly change the balance of power within the Party. Originally all the leaders had agreed to an early congress, but later Muzorewa and Sithole wanted a delay. Both Nkomo and Sithole aspired to replace Muzorewa as President, Nkomo remembering the strength of his popular support in 1964, Sithole hoping to capitalise on the success of the ZANU guerillas. ZAPU had kept some kind of skeleton organisation going in Rhodesia since PCC had been banned and was confident that a majority of delegates from the existing ANC branches would choose Nkomo as leader. ZAPU had put its efforts into recruiting guerillas and therefore had to build up its internal organisation before it could confidently compete against Nkomo.[18] Muzorewa probably recognised Nkomo as a distinct threat to his leadership and with Sithole's connivance delayed calling the congress. Nkomo's supporters grew increasingly aggrieved.

The animosity which had been building up tore ANC apart in September 1975, when, after mutual recriminations, Muzorewa expelled Nkomo from the Party and Nkomo held his own congress where he was elected President. The result was that two rival parties now existed: ANC (Muzorewa) and ANC (Nkomo). The hostility caused by competition for power between the leaders was reinforced by disagreement about the best policy to adopt after the abortive Victoria Falls meeting in August 1975 between representatives of ANC and the Government. Muzorewa, Sithole, and Chikerema believed that further discussions with Smith were futile, while Nkomo was prepared to try again. Nkomo remained in Rhodesia, while the other leaders exiled themselves in Zambia. The gulf between the two factions widened when Nkomo's party started formal constitutional discussions with the Government in November 1975. Nkomo's supporters hoped that Smith might now concede the substance of majority rule in return for certain minor concessions to the white minority. Muzorewa and his allies denounced Nkomo for betraying the Africans, but the breakdown of the constitutional talks in March 1976 showed that Nkomo was not prepared to sacrifice his principles to gain a settlement.

While Muzorewa and Nkomo opposed each other within Rhodesia, another group of nationalists, some of the ZANU guerillas, were effectively establishing themselves as a third independent unit outside the country. Several of the prominent commanders never accepted the authority of ANC and continued to fight as members of ZANU. Most ZANU guerillas refused to accept the proffered leadership of any ANC politician. Many recruits who went abroad in 1975 regarded Muzorewa as their leader, but he had had nothing to do with the ZANU guerillas already in the field. Chikerema was unacceptable as the ex-leader of FROLIZI and Nkomo remained anathema as the traditional enemy. Sithole had assumed that on his release from detention he would be able to convert his nominal Presidency of the ZANU guerillas into effective leadership, but they did not accept him. Although Sithole had tried to express the guerillas' frustration with the ceasefire, which formed part of the Lusaka Agreement, many rejected him because he had signed the Agreement, no matter how reluctantly.

Several in the ZANU High Command, in addition, seem by 1975 to have been hostile to control of the military by any politicians who had been national leaders of ZANU since 1963. A fierce quarrel had broken out in ZANU in Zambia at the end of 1974, which led to many political killings and culminated in March 1975 in the murder of Herbert Chitepo, the Chairman of the Dare, the War Council, and the most senior ZANU leader in Zambia. The facts of the case are contested, but one strand of the feud seems to have been antagonism between commanders, like Josiah Tongogara, with military training, but with no experience of politics within Rhodesia, and politicians, like Chitepo and Simpson Mutambanengwe, who had no military expertise, but who had been elected in 1964 to lead the party within Rhodesia. Some of the military commanders accused some of the political leaders of siding with a group of guerilla mutineers who had complained about the incompetence and corruption of the High Command. After the internecine fighting within ZANU and the arrest of many guerillas, including Tongogara himself, by the Zambian police following the death of Chitepo, many ZANU military men probably preferred to manage without political chiefs.[19] Sithole's bid for leadership of the ZANU guerillas came, then, at an inopportune moment.

Although many ZANU guerillas from early 1975 to early 1976 acknowledged no leader but Tongogara, or, while he was imprisoned in Zambia, another guerilla leader, Rex Nhongo, Mugabe eventually succeeded in putting himself at the head of the ZANU guerilla movement, where Sithole and the other politicians had failed. Mugabe was ambitious: when he and most of the other members of the ZANU Executive were in detention, he tried to oust Sithole from the leadership,[20] but the Zambian Government recognised Sithole as President in the negotiations leading to the Lusaka Agreement. Mugabe left Rhodesia in 1975 in an attempt to make himself leader of the ZANU forces in the field. At first he was unsuccessful and for some time was imprisoned in Mozambique. During 1976, however, he did succeed, in spite of his unmilitary background, in becoming a leader of the ZANU guerillas. Initally, at least, the military leaders seemed anxious not to abandon their autonomy and probably accepted Mugabe as a representative of their views in international forums rather than as an official entitled to command them.

The alliance of Mugabe and the ZANU guerillas became important for the first time at the Geneva Conference, which met from October to December 1976, another major event in the history of Rhodesian African nationalism that was, like the Lusaka Agreement, engineered from outside. This time, the improbable *deus ex machina* was Henry Kissinger, the United States Secretary of State, who, anxious to keep Russian influence from spreading in Southern Africa, decided to seek a solution to the Rhodesian problem. He persuaded the South African Government to exert further pressure on Smith, which John Vorster could easily do, since the only railways still carrying traffic into and out of Rhodesia ran into South Africa. In September 1976 Smith, obliged to abandon his defence of white minority power, declared that he would grant majority rule in two years time. To work out the details of a new constitution the Rhodesian

Government and the nationalist parties were invited to a conference in Geneva under the chairmanship of Ivor Richard, representing Britain.

Four separate African delegations went to Geneva, because, in addition to the parties led by Muzorewa, Nkomo, and Mugabe, there was now another one which had been founded in September 1976 by Sithole. He was probably tired of playing second-in-command to the less experienced Muzorewa and hoped to re-constitute the old ZANU.

As if in compensation for the fresh division in the nationalists' ranks, however, two of the parties, under Nkomo and Mugabe, decided, just before the Geneva Conference, to form an alliance called the Patriotic Front. Neither party wished to lose its identity, but each hoped to gain strength from working with the other. Nkomo and Mugabe were unlikely collaborators, but their association, in spite of severe strains, survived until 1979 and at the Lancaster House Conference appeared stronger than ever. Mugabe probably recognised the status that Nkomo enjoyed in Rhodesia and in the international community as the 'father' of African nationalism in Rhodesia, having been President of the Congress before Sithole, Mugabe, or Muzorewa had become members of the movement. More important, Nkomo's lieutenants had built up a good organisation in Rhodesia since their release from detention in December 1974, whereas Mugabe, who had been out of Rhodesia since 1975, had only an embryonic organisation within the country. Nkomo presumably hoped to gain from association with the ZANU guerilla army, which in 1976 was vastly increasing the scale of its onslaught on Rhodesia. Only after the failure of his negotiations with Smith in March 1976 did Nkomo start purposefully to build up the ZAPU guerilla force, which had been relatively insignificant. When he joined the Patriotic Front, Nkomo's guerilla army was not as big as Mugabe's and had made little impact within Rhodesia. The alliance between Nkomo and Mugabe was a strange marriage of convenience, especially as Nkomo was supported by the multi-national company, Lonrho, and Mugabe had adopted Marxist-Leninist-Maoism. Personally too the men were marked contrasts: Nkomo imprecise and jovial, Mugabe intellectual and ascetic.

After the failure of the Geneva Conference it was Smith's particular method of seeking a settlement that widened the rift between Muzorewa and Sithole on one side and the Patriotic Front on the other. The Geneva Conference did not secure agreement on a new constitution and on the transitional arrangements, because the African leaders demanded more than Smith had agreed with Kissinger to concede, and because Richard was unable to persuade Smith to accept British proposals that aimed to bridge the gap between the Rhodesian Front and the nationalists. In the first part of 1977 Smith seemed to hope that he might still escape from redeeming his pledge to Kissinger. Meanwhile the British and United States Governments produced the Anglo-American Plan for a Rhodesian settlement. Smith resented this intervention, but, recognising by the end of 1977 that he needed to make large concessions to the Africans in order to try and stop the guerilla war and have sanctions lifted, went ahead with his own plans for an 'internal' settlement. The Patriotic Front, hoping to win power by guerilla warfare, would not compromise with Smith, but Muzorewa and Sithole were ready to talk. They did not acknowledge it, but they, unlike Nkomo and Mugabe, were not recognised as leaders by any substantial, organised bodies of guerillas. Both had become of necessity internal leaders, seeking support at home. Muzorewa had returned to Rhodesia just before the Geneva Conference and Sithole came back in July 1977. By contrast, Mugabe operated permanently from Mozambique and Nkomo now had his headquarters in Zambia. At the end of 1977 the internal leaders started talks with Smith about a compromise constitution. Two years before Nkomo had had constitutional discussions with Smith, while Muzorewa and Sithole denounced him from outside the country. Now the positions were reversed.

The internal settlement in March 1978 between Smith, Muzorewa, Sithole, and Chief Chirau, whom Smith had at one stage taken into his Government and who now led a party called ZUPO (Zimbabwe United People's Organisation), caused greater hostility between segments of the nationalist movement than anything previously in its tortured history. The Patriotic Front maintained that the white minority would preserve its power under the new constitution and that Muzorewa and Sithole were mere puppets. They, on the other hand, argued that they had secured the basic nationalist ends of one man, one vote, and majority rule, and that their concessions to the Europeans were desirable in order to persuade experienced white people to continue contributing to the administration and the economy of the country. In the internal settlement Smith yielded universal franchise and a black-dominated government, but gained twenty-eight seats out of an assembly of a hundred for the Europeans, who numbered less than one-twentieth of the population. Furthermore, the Europeans were to have a veto on constitutional change for ten years, and the top jobs in the Civil Service, the judiciary, the police, and the army were to remain for the immediate future in white hands.

Until the first election under the new constitution, a transitional government was in power, in which white and black shared responsibility. This meant that Muzorewa and Sithole were now nominally in charge of the security forces who were fighting the Patriotic Front guerillas. Both Muzorewa and Sithole tried to persuade the guerillas to lay down their arms now that the nationalist goals had been achieved, but most guerillas ignored the offer of an amnesty. The hatred between the Patriotic Front and the black parties in the transitional government was exacerbated by Muzorewa and Sithole setting up their own private armies, the auxiliaries. These soldiers both aided the regular security forces and provided the black political leaders in government with their personal military bases. Now that Muzorewa and Sithole were engaged in open war with Mugabe and Nkomo, the receding prospects of reconciliation retreated more rapidly.

The election in April 1979 deepened the rift. Nkomo threatened to bomb the polling stations, but security was tight enough to permit 64 per cent of the estimated black electorate to vote. The Patriotic Front believed that the election was not free and some observers claimed that intimidation by the security forces, the auxiliaries, and white employers accounted for the high turn-out. Most observers, however, thought that the election was reasonably fair and, if many people had gone unwillingly to vote, one would have expected a higher proportion of spoilt ballot papers than the actual 3.55 per cent of the total poll. For Muzorewa the election was a substantial victory, as he received 67.27 per cent of the vote and fifty-one out of the seventy-two black seats.[21] He now became Prime Minister of a coalition government in which, as the constitution prescribed, all parties were entitled to be represented in proportion to the number of seats that they won in the election. This meant that Muzorewa's UANC colleagues were working in government with Rhodesian Front Ministers. This continued collaboration between UANC and the traditional enemy of the African nationalists reinforced the enmity of the Patriotic Front to the African parties of the internal settlement.

The election also precipitated further divisions among the internal nationalists. Sithole, who had worked with Muzorewa to obtain the internal settlement and in the Executive Council of the transitional government, claimed that the election was unfair and the results invalid. Consequently his party refused at first to take their seats in parliament. More damaging to Muzorewa was the defection from UANC of eight newly-elected members of parliament in June 1979 in protest against Muzorewa's autocratic rule. They formed a new party, ZDP, under Chikerema. He had a special personal grievance against Muzorewa, because he had been placed, in spite of his seniority in the movement, in the last place on UANC's list of election candidates for Mashonaland West, which meant that, if UANC had polled insufficient votes in this area for all their candidates to obtain seats, Chikerema would not have been in parliament. The loss of eight members to ZDP meant that Muzorewa no longer had a majority of seats in the Assembly.

The Patriotic Front, although united in attacking the Muzorewa Government and in negotiating with the British Government at the Lancaster House constitutional conference, which started in September 1979, had its own internal problems. By 1978 Nkomo had built up a formidable guerilla army in Zambia of at least eight thousand men, who were believed to be better trained and equipped than the ZANU guerillas who had since 1972 borne the main burden of the fighting. Yet Nkomo still committed relatively few of his guerillas to the war within Rhodesia, which caused resentment in some ZANU leaders. Even within ZAPU itself there was disagreement, sometimes reportedly violent, about whether the Party should play a more active part in the war. An important cause of stress within the Patriotic Front was Nkomo's meeting with Smith in August 1978 without informing Mugabe. Elements in ZANU were afraid that Nkomo might be trying to do a deal with Smith at ZANU's expense, although Nkomo had hoped to have a further meeting with Smith at which Mugabe would be present. The mutual suspicion between the leaders was reflected in relations between the rank and file guerillas. Fighting sometimes took place between bands of ZAPU and ZANU soldiers.[22] Against this background of suspicions and resentments, ZANU and ZAPU made periodic moves towards merging into a single party, but the resistance to this, especially in ZANU, proved too great. One of the subjects of a serious dispute in ZANU in 1977–78, which led to the imprisonment of a large group of dissidents, some of them senior officials, was whether to merge with ZAPU.[23] This splitting over unity was reminiscent of the arguments within ZANU and ZAPU in 1971, which led to the formation of FROLIZI.

III

The analysis of African nationalist development so far has shown how the proliferations of parties and the divisions within them can be largely explained by non-tribal factors like dissatisfaction with leaders, e.g., with Nkomo in 1963 and Chikerema in 1970, and ambition for power, e.g., the desertion of Muzorewa by Nkomo, Mugabe, and Sithole in 1975–76. The question to be faced now is how important tribe has been in providing further motives for the quarrels.

Some people have suspected that the first major split in the nationalist movement, in 1963, which led to the formation of ZANU, was based on tribe. Nkomo's PCC/ZAPU, it has been argued, received its support predominantly from the Ndebele-speaking people, while Sithole's ZANU drew its members mainly from those who spoke one of the Shona dialects. This can be answered by pointing out that the division resulted initially from a quarrel within the National Executive of ZAPU about the quality of Nkomo's leadership. The nationalist leaders' motives for forming two parties were not ostensibly tribal, nor were the appeals that they made for support. Neither PCC nor ZANU drew all its leaders from one tribal grouping. Nkomo, who is Ndebele, included among his lieutenants fellow Ndebele, like Moyo and Silundika, but he also chose Shona, like Chikerema and Willie Musarurwa. The ZANU Executive was predominantly Shona, but Enos Nkala was Ndebele and Sithole himself, although Shona on his father's side, was brought up in his mother's family in Matabeleland speaking Ndebele. A more significant factor than tribe in determining whether the most senior leaders left Nkomo seems to have been the date when they joined the movement. Those who had worked with Nkomo since 1957, when the Congress was established, or before, like Nyandoro and Moyo, stayed with him, while those who had become nationalist leaders only in 1960, like Sithole and Mugabe, joined ZANU. It might have been the case that, although the leaders were not tribally motivated, the mass of the people divided between PCC and ZANU according to tribe. It is certainly true that ZANU was particularly strong in the Shona, eastern districts round Umtali and Fort Victoria, while PCC had a heavy majority in the Ndebele area round Bulawayo. In and around Salisbury, however, where the Shona heavily outnumbered the Ndebele, Nkomo was distinctly more popular than Sithole. In the country at large Nkomo had a distinct edge, although the Ndebele formed only about a fifth of the African population.

One of the paradoxes of Rhodesian nationalist politics is that tribe has seemed a more divisive factor abroad than at home. Strong prima facie cases can be made that tribe was a significant cause of the conflicts within ZAPU in 1970–71 and in ZANU in 1974–75. These quarrels were the fiercest and most violent in the history of the movement. Both took place in Zambia between guerilla leaders and between guerillas. All the disputants and combatants were living away from their tribal homes, but appeared to be moved by tribal motives. Leaders and followers who had not been influenced by tribal rivalries when living in Rhodesia seemed to generate tribal hostility when living abroad.

The disruption within ZAPU in 1970 had many causes, but tribalism seemed to play a part. The rival groups of leaders came from different tribes: Chikerema and Nyandoro were Shona, Moyo and Silundika were Ndebele. Each side accused the other of tribal conspiracy. Chikerema claimed that Moyo's original document in the paper war between them was 'intended to protect clans, and tribal corruption in the Party and Army', and spoke of 'dark tribal secret meetings'.[24] Moyo retaliated by accusing Chikerema of contributing to the crisis in the party by private meetings with members of his own tribe.[25] Neither the fact that the leaders were members of different tribes, nor the fact that they accused each other of tribal partiality proves that either set of leaders was fundamentally motivated by tribal hostility, although clearly the awareness of tribal differences inflamed the political animosity. However, the guerillas themselves do appear to have divided into Shona and Ndebele factions, who fought each other.[26] Some Shona also attacked Moyo and Silundika, while Nyandoro was given police protection because he thought that he was being hunted down by Ndebele soldiers.[27]

When FROLIZI formed in 1971, both ZAPU and ZANU accused the new organisation of being a Zezuru clique. The Zezuru are a group of Shona living around Salisbury, who speak similar Shona dialects. The accusation was based on the fact that the most prominent leaders, including Chikerema and Nyandoro from ZAPU and Nathan Shamuyarira from ZANU, were Zezuru.[28] However, it is almost literally incredible that a party whose overt purpose was to re-unite ZAPU and ZANU in a national organisation should covertly be acting in the interest of a Shona sub-division.

The case that the severe disputes within ZANU in 1974–75 were largely the product of tribal hostilities was presented in detail in the *Report* of the international commission set up by the Zambian Government to investigate the circumstances of Chitepo's death.[29] The *Report* assumed rather than argued that the linguistic sub-divisions of the Shona had distinct political interests, and attributed much of the trouble within the ZANU guerilla movement to the political ambition of a group of Karanga, led by Tongogara. A group of ZANU members, who sympathised with Tongogara and his associates, published a rejoinder to the international commission's *Report,* in which they showed the weakness of some of the evidence that was advanced to prove the tribal rivalry.[30] The *Report* alleged that the 1971 elections to the Dare, the War Council, strengthened the Manyika, to whom the Karanga were supposed to be opposed, but the evidence that the *Report* itself provided shows that the Manyika were no stronger in 1971 than in the previous Dare. It therefore made no sense for the *Report* to say that 'the Karanga elements more than ever intensified the struggle to correct the imbalance in the Dare and to establish their ascendancy'.[31] The *Report* is again wrong when it states that the Karanga won a majority in the elections to the Dare in 1973, for, as Tongogara's allies showed, the Karanga numbered only four out of eight. The *Report* had the figures wrong, because it called a Zezuru member a Karanga.[32] The ZANU critics argued convincingly that 'it would be far more relevant to look at the ages, political principles and background of the new leaders than to look at their tribes', and provided non-tribal reasons for the changes in the Dare in 1973.[33] The heart of the international commission's case was that a group of Karanga led by Tongogara tried to move a group of Manyika led by Chitepo from power within ZANU by the use of force, which resulted in the death of two Manyika leaders, Chitepo and John Mataure. Most of those who acted with Tongogara were Karanga, but some, like Joseph Chimurenga and Rex Nhongo, were not. In any case, the fact that some political allies came from the same tribal groupings does not prove that they worked together *because* of this. Whether the Tongogara group was basically tribal or not, it certainly believed that its opponents were a tribal clique, that some of the Manyika had organised themselves into an exclusively Manyika faction, which inspired a mutiny in the guerilla army.[34] Of course, the belief in a Manyika conspiracy, although providing a motive of action for the Tongogara group, does not of itself prove that such a conspiracy did in fact exist, although several of Chitepo's political associates, like Noel Mukono, were Manyika. As in the ZAPU crisis of 1970–71, there were more accusations and suspicions of tribalism than concrete evidence of tribal scheming or favouritism.[35]

Between the conflict within ZANU in 1974–75 and Chikerema's quarrel with Muzorewa in 1979 the signs of tribal hostility within or between parties were few, although some observers would still want to explain the support for different leaders by tribal loyalties. The ZANU guerillas do seem to be overwhelmingly Shona and the ZAPU guerillas seem, correspondingly, to be heavily Ndebele, although hard evidence of the tribal composition of the guerilla armies is not available. The parties at home permit less neat tribal classification. Tribe seems an irrelevance to most of the national party leaders. Both Muzorewa and Nkomo, when his party was legal within the country, until 1978, worked with tribally mixed Central Committees. Nkomo, who is sometimes presented as the Ndebele leader, trusts Shona, Josiah Chinamano and Joseph Msika, as his right-hand men. If the leaders of each party are tribe-blind, and tribally mixed, then it is somewhat surprising if their supporters try to choose a party simply on tribal grounds. A Ndebele might be attracted to ZAPU because Nkomo is President, but he has then to come to terms with the fact that Nkomo takes advice from Shona. Nevertheless, Nkomo has been stronger in the Ndebele areas than elsewhere. His support in the Shona area round Salisbury has been distinctly weaker than Muzorewa's, but it is doubtful if this can be attributed simply to tribal prejudice. In 1964 Nkomo was very popular in the Salisbury district, but when he was released from detention in 1974 and returned to active politics he found that Muzorewa had, in his absence, for many people taken over his role as national symbol of the African nationalist movement. With the very rapid population increase, a large number of young Africans had grown to political consciousness between 1964 and 1974 who had no experience of Nkomo as anything but an absent martyr. His tribal pull did seem to enable Nkomo to regain his predominance in Matabeleland, but his attempts to replace Muzorewa seemed to many in Mashonaland to be disloyalty to the national leader.

What is almost cetainly wrong is to assume that support for the competing African leaders is given *solely* on tribal grounds and that support for each party is restricted to a particular tribe or tribes. UANC, in particular, was widely popular in the 1979 election. Muzorewa gained over two-thirds of the national vote and won a not wholly derisory minority of the vote, 20 per cent, even in the electoral area, Matabeland South, where he did least well (compare Sithole's 7.2 per cent in his worst district, Mashonaland East). UANC was most successful in the three Mashonaland electoral areas round Salisbury, winning four-fifths of the vote, but it had a majority of votes in six out of the eight areas and came top of the poll in a seventh, Matabeleland North, with 40.84 per cent of the votes. The official election statistics do not give the voting by tribe, but by districts within the eight larger electoral areas. It is, therefore, not possible to generalise with certainty about how the tribes divided their votes, but a reasonable hypothesis is that Muzorewa had *some* support from most tribes. The theory that he was strongest in Mashonaland for tribal reasons does not hold up, because Muzorewa, a Manyika, appears to have attracted strong support from Zezuru and Korekore.[36]

The strongest case that can be made that tribe affected voting behaviour in 1979 rests on the support in the Ndebele areas for Chief Kayisa Ndiweni's UNFP (United National Federal Party). He did have a little support all over the country and his success in the two Matabeleland areas was much less spectacular (two-fifths of the vote) than Muzorewa's in Mashonaland, but he was clearly a tribal candidate in a way that neither Muzorewa nor Sithole were. He resigned from the transitional government because his plan for the Ndebele to have half the seats in parliament was rejected. (It was a ridiculous proposal, since the Ndebele constituted only a fifth of the population.) In the election campaign he called for a federal system of government in which the Ndebele and the Shona would each have a degree of home rule. It is thus reasonable to infer that some Ndebele voted for his party, because they felt that it would specially guard their interests.[37]

After the 1979 election two new parties were founded that had some appearance of having tribal bases, Chikerema's ZDP and Michael Mawema's NFZ. Immediately after the election Chikerema complained of tribalism and nepotism in the nomination of parliamentary candidates in UANC and accused Muzorewa of running a tribal mafia. UANC retaliated when Chikerema led seven other members of parliament out of UANC to form ZDP by calling the new party a Zwimba clique.[38] Most of them came originally from the Zwimba Tribal Trust Land. This does not, however, prove that they were in favour of a narrow tribal sectionalism. At least ostensibly, they were opposing tribalism, or what they interpreted as tribalism, not endorsing it.

The founding of NFZ in November 1979 lends some credibility to the view that tribe had become increasingly important in the black politics of Zimbabwe Rhodesia. Michael Mawema, the President of NFZ, was reported as saying that eighty per cent of the people would vote on tribal lines at the next election.[39] He was invited to form a new party by influential Karanga. One of the main short-term objectives of NFZ was to obtain the release of about a hundred members of Mugabe's ZANU from detention within Mozambique, who were said to be Karanga. In 1977 and 1978 Mugabe arrested some members of the ZANU Central Committee, including Rugare Gumbo and Matuku Hamadziripi, and many officers and men from the guerilla army. The dissidents had many grievances, some ideological. They also objected that decisions of the Central Committee could be easily vetoed by the military leadership, that not all the members of the Central Committee, including Mugabe, had been elected, and that some leaders had resisted moves towards merging with ZAPU.[40] Those imprisoned did not regard themselves as the victims of tribal prejudice, so it is by no means certain that those who demanded their release were moved primarily by tribal solidarity. Those who knew or lived near the imprisoned men might have a special sympathy for their plight, although this would not necessarily amount to tribalism. It is difficult to see the relevance of Karanga loyalism in this particular case, since one of the dissidents' main opponents was Tongogara, who is himself a Karanga and who was accused by the international commission of leading a Karanga faction in 1974–75. If Karangas did want a leader from their own tribe, they could follow either Tongogara or Gumbo and Mawema. In any case, none of these leaders aimed at purely Karanga support. Mawema found justification for the establishment of ZNP in the widespread disappointment of Africans in Zimbabwe Rhodesia with the failure of the Muzorewa Government to bring peace and prosperity and with the inability of Mugabe's ZANU to control the brutality of his guerillas.[41]

IV

Even when a prima facie case exists that tribe was influential in a particular episode in the African politics of Zimbabwe Rhodesia, a problem may still exist about *why* and *how* tribe affected political behaviour. Furthermore, any general theory about the importance of tribe has to take account of the fact that the word 'tribe' is used differently in different contexts, for example, sometimes to mean all the Shona-speaking people, at other times to mean only those subject to a particular chief's jurisdiction. Explanation of political rivalries by tribal allegiances may create more problems that it solves, as tribe is rarely an easily intelligible cause of nationalist divisions.

Since tribes existed before the Europeans came, it is natural to assume that pre-colonial conflict affected relations between Africans in modern politics. When the Europeans began the colony of Southern Rhodesia in the 1890s, strained relations existed between the centralised military state of the Ndebele, who lived round Bulawayo, and the neighbouring Shona chiefdoms, whose lands the Ndebele periodically raided. The white settlers have believed that the traditional hostility between Ndebele and Shona has persisted into modern African politics. This theory, however, has several weaknesses. The first is that the wars between the Ndebele and the Shona are ancient history and have gradually faded from the folk memory. The British South Africa Company, which ruled Southern Rhodesia in the early years of the colony, destroyed the military monarchy of the Ndebele in the war of 1893 and thus ended the killing and plundering expeditions of the Ndebele warriors. The enmity of each tribe for the other tended to be superseded by the resentment of both at European domination. In 1896 both Shona and Ndebele rebelled against white rule and there was some degree of coordination between them.[42]

The idea that the modern Shona and Ndebele inherited an historical hatred of each other is further undermined by the fact that neither tribe was an undifferentiated social unit when the Europeans came. The Ndebele state was highly integrated by the rule of an authoritarian king acting through a military hierarchy, but within the society there were marked divisions of caste. The two superior castes, the Zansi and the Enhla, were descended from the Nguni people who originally invaded the Bulawayo area around 1840. The lowest caste, the Lowzi or Holi, were descendants of the original Shona inhabitants of the district who were conquered and absorbed into the Ndebele state. Those African leaders in the nationalist movement who are often loosely called 'Ndebele', like Nkomo and Silundika, are from this third caste and are more strictly described as Kalanga. Although they speak Ndebele, they are descended from the original Shona of western Zimbabwe Rhodesia.[43] The Kalanga would be less likely to identify themselves with the military exploits of the Ndebele against the Shona than the descendents of the pure Ndebele aristocracy. These, however, have played no significant part in nationalist politics.[44]

The Shona were much less united when the Europeans colonised Southern Rhodesia than the inhabitants of the Ndebele lands. The Shona did not form a single cohesive society or state. The Africans who belonged to the various chiefdoms that made up the Shona could be regarded as one tribal grouping because they had similar languages, cultures and political systems. There had in the distant past been empires, like that of the Rowzi Mambos, which ended in the 1830s and which embraced many, although not all, Shona, but in the 1890s the Shona lived in many separate societies under many separate chiefly jurisdictions.[45] Not all the Shona suffered from Ndebele raids and those that did suffered unequally. The Shona groups did not all have the same reason to hate the Ndebele, whose raids were not viewed as a challenge to the Shona as a whole. In the 1890s the Shona lacked a sense of Shona identity.[46] The notion that the Shona in modern politics are re-living an historical antipathy to the Ndebele is, therefore, based on a misleadingly simplistic version of African history.[47]

Sometimes tribal interpretations of nationalist politics depend less on an imagined hostility between Shona and Ndebele than on the six sub-divisions of the Shona: Zezuru, Manyika, Korekore, Karanga, Ndau, and Kalanga. These groups did not, however, form integrated social or political units, any more than the Shona as a whole. The six sub-divisions are linguistic, each group of people speaking related dialects of Shona. There tend to be cultural and ethnic similaries within these linguistic sub-divisions of the Shona, but there is not an exact correspondence between the divisions of the Shona according to dialect and the divisions according to customs. Since the linguistic groupings were never politically integrated, there were no historical conflicts to inspire modern rivalries.[48]

The cohesive political and social units among the Shona before the Europeans arrived and since were the clans, like the Zwimba or the Shawasha, each under its own chief. The elected chief had ritual and judicial jurisdiction over a group of wards or communities, each of which contained several villages.[49] When Africans say which tribe they come from, they refer to a clan, not a linguistic sub-division. For example, Didymus Mutasa, now a supporter of Mugabe, said in his book that he is descended on his father's side from the Makoni tribe, and Muzorewa in his autobiography said that he came from the Makombe clan.[50] If traditional social and political units were to form a basis for modern political loyalties, these clans would be significant. However, only rarely have they been used to explain political divisions within the nationalist movement. The exception that proves the rule is the accusation that ZDP was a Zwimba clique.

A further difficulty in trying to tie modern political divisions to traditional tribal groupings is that the process of European colonisation has tended to erode tribal life. Many Africans who worked in European mines, farms, factories, and homes left their tribal homes temporarily or permanently. The African townships, which grew up outside European cities, were mixed tribal communities. Urban Africans tended to become alienated from their tribal values. Many Africans learnt sufficiently fluent English to be able to talk to any other Africans whom they met, irrespective of tribe. Indeed, the breakdown of tribal separation was a necessary condition for the growth of a nationalist movement, which aimed at a country-wide membership and emphasised the existence of a single Zimbabwe nation.

It is paradoxical to seek tribal divisions within the nationalist movement, because the intention of all the nationalists was, of course, to transcend, or even obliterate, tribe in the quest to build or strengthen the African nation. Those, like Mugabe, who have incorporated Marxism into their nationalism have a further motive for repudiating tribe, for they analyse the nationalist struggle in class terms. No nationalist could act tribally and remain consistent with his nationalist principles.[51]

Conflicts between principle and practice are common in politics, but many of the nationalist leaders had their intentions to make tribe politically irrelevant reinforced by their experiences as politicians and, sometimes, professional men. Some have been educated or have worked abroad. Some have lived in exile because their parties have been banned in Zimbabwe Rhodesia. Men like Enoch Dumbutshena, a lawyer who lived in Zambia for twelve years, and Stanlake Samkange, a university historian who lived in the United States for a similar period,[52] seem of all Africans the least likely to dabble in tribalism, although both were accused of being part of a Zwimba clique in 1979, and Dumbutshena was allegedly a member of a Zezuru clique in 1971. It strains credibility that the most sophisticated, cosmopolitan Africans should behave in the most parochial fashion. Even those nationalist leaders who have spent less time abroad have not lived in their tribal homelands, except when confined there by government restriction order in 1962. They have worked with nationalist colleagues of varying tribes in environments inimical to tribal particularism: in restriction camps and in prison; in party headquarters in Salisbury (significantly Nkomo's parties have operated from the capital, not Bulawayo, amidst the Ndebele); in exile in Lusaka and Maputo.

A significant, although admittedly not conclusive, argument against the prevalence of tribalism in the politics of Zimbabwe Rhodesia is that the nationalist leaders never acknowledged that they themselves had tribal motives and usually denied that tribalism was a serious problem in the nationalist movement.[53] They treated tribalism as a political sin, which they often attributed to opponents.[54] Calling an opponent a tribalist was a way of disparaging him, like calling him an imperialist.[55] *The Zimbabwe Star* of 29 November 1975, for example, commenting on behalf of Nkomo's ANC about the attempts of Muzorewa, Sithole, and Chikerema to obtain guerilla support abroad, quoted 'close sources' as saying: 'the freedom fighters regard the presence of these tribalists ... as a threat to a future free Zimbabwe'. Sometimes the accusations of tribalism were not pure abuse, but based on genuine suspicion. In 1976 leaders in Nkomo's ANC believed that Edson Sithole, one of Muzorewa's lieutenants, was unscrupulously stirring up tribal feeling among uneducated Shona against Nkomo for political purposes.[56]

Fear of others' tribalism, even if it is in fact unfounded, has itself sometimes been a powerful motive for acting against colleagues within the nationalist movement. During the crises within ZAPU in 1970–71, in ZANU in 1974–75, and when ZDP left UANC in 1979 fears of tribalism seem to have been genuine. Such fears did not themselves constitute tribalism, but they contributed to widening divisions within the movement.[57]

On occasion fear of tribal wrangling led nationalist politicians to try to forestall it. Sithole deliberately appointed two from each of the six Shona sub-divisions and two Ndebele to the national executive of his ZANU in March 1977, in order to prevent the quarrels that had taken place in ZANU in 1974–75, which he blamed on tribal imbalance in the Central Committee.[58] Muzorewa in May 1979 sponsored a Ndebele rather than a fellow Manyika for the office of President in the new government of Zimbabwe Rhodesia, because he, the future Prime Minister, was a Manyika and he was anxious for tribal balance.[59] The expression of fears in this way may in fact create rather than allay suspicions of tribalism, for such preventative actions suggest that there is something to be prevented.

Tribalism, perhaps, is a will-o'-the-wisp, which has been chased, but has little substance. If tribalism were genuine and based on long established social divisions, its appearance would be more constant than it has actually been. In its various manifestations, as Shona-Ndebele rivalry, divisions within the Shona, or the ambition of a clan, it surfaces suddenly and disappears. Different parties have different tribal crises in different years. This suggests that many forms of 'tribalism' do not have deep roots. People who are accused of tribalism today may have appeared innocent of it yesterday and may again look innocent tomorrow. Tongogara's career as a Karanga factionalist, for example, did not seem to survive the early 1970s. The political collaboration of particular men, which is regarded as healthy for the movement in one period of its development, may seem sinister in another. Chikerema, who was born at Kutama Mission, forty miles east of Salisbury, and Nyandoro, who was born in Chiota Reserve, thirty miles to the south of Salisbury,[60] were admired in the late 1950s for working together to build the nationalist movement, but in 1970–71 their opponents reviled them as first Shona and then Zezuru tribalists.

Much of the popular support for particular leaders which has been attributed to tribalism may have been, more simply, regionalism, which has less menacing overtones. People may know, or know of, leaders who have lived or worked locally, whether or not, in any sense, they come from the same tribe. Not merely in Zimbabwe Rhodesia people take pride in the achievements of local men. The fame of Chitepo as the first African barrister probably helped to build ZANU support in the area near his birthplace, near Inyanga in the east, when he joined the Party in 1963.[61] It is difficult to know how widely a leader's popularity stretches from the particular place with which he is associated. Sithole, interestingly, had colossal support in the 1979 Election in the Chipinga electoral district (43,694 to UANC's 3,442), which includes Mount Selinda, where he was principal of a school from 1958 to 1960 and near where he had a farm from 1961. He did much less well in the Melsetter district, which is quite close and contains many members of his 'tribe', the Ndau (7,568 to UANC's 3,511).[62] The popularity of Msika in Bulawayo in a succession of nationalist parties indicates the importance of local rather than tribal support, because Msika lived and worked in Bulawayo, where the population is mainly Ndebele, but he was a Shona born in Chiweshe Reserve, near Salisbury.

The burden of the argument has been to suggest that tribe as a factor in African politics has been a myth. It should, however, perhaps be conceded that myths may help to create realities. Just as fears of tribalism may deepen political rifts, whether or not there is any tribalism to be afraid of, so the myth of tribe, however conceived, may contribute to the establishment of a new political grouping. Professor Ranger writes: 'Those who now feel themselves to be Kore-Kore or Zezuru or Karanga are likely to be . . . unimpressed by a historian's protestation that they can't be.' He believes that there are now in the politics of Zimbabwe Rhodesia 'newly invented "tribes" '.[63] It is a hypothesis to be tested. If new 'tribes' exist, the meaning of 'tribe' has still to be elucidated.

Unless party leaders favour their own tribe, however defined, in allocating jobs and resources, there seems no point in people voting tribally. There is little evidence that tribal favouritism is common in Zimbabwe Rhodesia, so any kind of tribal allegiance in political life remains difficult to explain or even believe in.

NOTES

1. I am grateful to the Nuffield Foundation and the Research Board of the University of Leicester for grants in support of research that has been used in this essay. Southern Rhodesia became Rhodesia in 1964 and Zimbabwe Rhodesia in 1979. I refer to it as Zimbabwe Rhodesia, except when dealing with a particular period before 1 June 1979, when I employ the name in use at the time.

2. *The Domboshawa 'Indaba': the Demand for Independence in Rhodesia* (Salisbury, Rhodesia, 1964), 50.

3. *The Washington Post,* 8 May 1977, c4. The article asserts that Mugabe and the ZANU guerrilla leader, Rex Nhongo, are Karanga, which they are not.

4. P. L. Moorcraft, *A Short Thousand Years: The End of Rhodesia's Rebellion* (Salisbury, 1979), 164.

5. *The Guardian,* 31 August 1977, 10. 'Matabele' is an alternative version of 'Ndebele'. See also N. Ashford, 'The crucial choice before Zimbabwe Rhodesia', *The Times,* 26 November 1979, 12, which claims that 'the tribal factor will, regrettably, be of far greater importance' to the outcome of the next election than party or ideological considerations.

6. *The Daily Telegraph,* 30 October 1979. The headline would have been more intelligible, although still misleading, if the report had mentioned the prediction by the NFZ leader that eighty per cent of the electorate would vote on tribal lines (Ashford, *loc. cit.*).

7. L. W. Bowman, *Politics in Rhodesia: White Power in an African State* (Cambridge, Mass., 1973), 50.

8. C. Palley, *Memorandum on the Rhodesian Election Campaign, on whether Elections were Fair and Free and whether Principles Required for Rhodesian Independence have been Satisfied* (Canterbury, 1979), 19.

9. C. Palley, *Zimbabwe Rhodesia: should the present government be recognised?* (London, 1979), quoted in T. Ranger, 'Rhodesia's politics of tribalism', 49 *New Society* (1979), 496–7.

10. *The Herald* (Salisbury), 25 April, 10, 11 May 1979. On Palley's hypothesis one would expect Muzorewa to have received few votes in the Bulawayo electoral district, but he actually received 68,113 out of 149,639 cast. The official figures, which show how electoral districts voted, not how tribes voted, suggest a more complex tribal distribution than Palley suggests.

11. R. Molteno, 'Cleavage and conflict in Zambian politics: a study in sectionalism' in W. Tordoff (ed.), *Politics in Zambia* (Manchester, 1974), 62–106.

12. *Op. cit.,* 96. T. Rasmussen, 'Political competition and one-party dominance in Zambia', 7 *Journal of Modern African Studies* (1969), 419.

13. J. Day, 'Southern Rhodesian African Nationalists and the 1961 Constitution', 7 *Journal of Modern African Studies* (1969), 221–47.

14. Day, *International Nationalism* (London, 1967), 19–22, 112–18.

15. J. R. D. Chickerema, *Reply to Observations on Our Struggle* (Lusaka, 1970); interview with M. Malianga, 4 May 1976.

16. For Nkomo's account of the split, see his Cold Comfort Farm speech, 10 August 1963, printed in 2 *Zimbabwe Review* (Cairo), August-September 1963. For a ZANU version of events, see N. Shamuyarira, *Crisis in Rhodesia* (London, 1965), 173–84.

17. J. Z. Moyo, *Observations on Our Struggle* (Lusaka, 1970); Chikerema, *op. cit.*; Moyo, *On the Coup Crisis Precipitated by J. Chikerema* (Lusaka, 1970).

18. Interview with M. Malianga, 4 May 1976.

19. *Report of the Special International Commission on the Assassination of Herbert Wiltshire Chitepo* (Lusaka, 1976); *The Price of Detente* (London, 1976); interviews with S. Mutambanengwe, 14 May 1976, G. Nyandoro, 12 May 1976, C. Sanyanga, 16 May 1976.

20. Interview with M. Malianga, 4 May 1976; R. Cary and D. Mitchell, *African Nationalist Leaders in Rhodesia Who's Who* (Bulawayo, Rhodesia, 1977), 170.

21. *The Herald,* 25 April 1979.

22. Interview by M. Gregory with G. Silundika, 25 September 1979, confirming reports by the security forces.

23. *The Truth about the Recurrent ZANU Crisis and the Emergence of a Two Line Struggle* (Mozambique, 1979), written by some of the detained leaders.
24. Chikerema, *op. cit.*
25. Moyo, *On the Coup Crisis.*
26. A. R. Wilkinson, *Insurgency in Rhodesia, 1957–1973: An Account and Assessment* (London, 1973), 21; K. Maxey, *The Fight for Zimbabwe: The armed conflict in Southern Rhodesia since UDI* (Brentwood, Essex, 1973), 16.
27. Maxey, *op. cit.*
28. B. Davidson, J. Slovo, A. R. Wilkinson, *Southern Africa: The New Politics of Revolution* (Harmondsworth, Middlesex, 1976), 249. Nyandoro in an interview, 12 May 1976, said that there were other tribes in FROLIZI, including Manyika.
29. *Report, op. cit.,* especially 11–13, 14, 26, 28, 29–30, 45–50.
30. *Price, op. cit.,* 5, 11–12.
31. *Report, op. cit.,* 11–12.
32. *Report, op. cit.,* 12–13; *Price, op. cit.,* 11.
33. *Price, op. cit.* Another weakness in the *Report* is its unproved assumption that the Shangana and the Karanga were allies because they came from contiguous areas (*Report, op. cit.,* 29–30, *Price, op. cit.*).
34. *Report, op. cit.,* 26, 28, 50. Tongogara's supporters who wrote *The Price of Detente,* although discounting the theory that the Karanga formed a tribal group aiming at political power, claimed that some Manyika did form an exclusive Manyika group, which re-awakened fears of tribal domination (*Price, op. cit.,* 2).
35. There is some feeling among the Karanga and among outsiders that the Karanga do form a distinctive tribal group. Some Karanga claim to be special because the ruins of Zimbabwe, with their reminders of past African achievements, are in their area. The Karanga have the reputation of being aggressive and many have served in the Rhodesian army and police. It is commonly believed that they form the majority of the ZANU guerilla army, although *The Price of Detente* (11) said that the Korekore were in a majority in 1974–75.
36. *The Herald,* 25 April, 10, 11 May 1979. It is a matter for speculation how Patriotic Front participation in the election would have affected Muzorewa's vote.
37. A member of parliament left Ndiweni's UNFP in August 1979 because, he alleged, it was riddled with tribalism and did not want Shona (*The Herald,* 29 August 1979).
38. *The Herald,* 24 April 1979.
39. Ashford, *op. cit.* Ashford also quotes Tendai Dumbushena (*sic,* Dumbutshena?), an African commentator: 'if you remove the element of coercion then most people will vote for people who are closest to them, in other words for members of the same tribe'.
40. *Truth, op. cit.*
41. *The Daily Telegraph,* 30 October 1979.
42. T. O. Ranger, *Revolt in Southern Rhodesia 1896–7* (London, 1967), 142–60.
43. H. Kuper, A. J. B. Hughes, J. van Velsen, *The Shona and Ndebele of Southern Rhodesia* (London, 1954), 44, 71–5.
44. According to G. Nyandoro (interview, 12 May 1976), the real Ndebele supported Muzorewa, not Nkomo.
45. Kuper *et al., op. cit.,* 17, 28–9; Ranger, *Revolt in Southern Rhodesia,* 9, 32.
46. D. Munjeri, an oral history interviewer in the Shona programme of the National Archives, Salisbury (*The Herald,* 29 June 1979).
47. In building a sense of nation nationalist leaders in the late 1950s and early 1960s invoked the memory of tribal heros from pre-colonial days. The Shona revered Chaminuka, who defied the Ndebele king, Lobengula; the Ndebele honoured Lobengula, the scourge of the Shona. Yet this use of tribal history did not divide the nationalist movement, nor create consciousness of separate tribal identities. See Shamuyarira, *op. cit.,* 28–30.
48. Kuper, *et al., op. cit.,* 10–13.
49. J. F. Holleman, *Chief, Council and Commissioner* (Assen, The Netherlands, 1968), 83–96; A. K. H. Weinrich, *Chiefs and Councils in Rhodesia* (London, 1971), 44–51.
50. D. Mutasa, *Rhodesian Black Behind Bars* (London, 1974), 14–15; Bishop A. T. Muzorewa, *Rise Up and Walk* (London, 1979), 2.

51. Chief Ndiweni made a blatantly tribal appeal, but he was not a nationalist. Like all the chiefs, he had been used by the white government as a bureaucratic instrument for controlling the Africans. The Rhodesian Front hoped to undermine support for the nationalists by adding to the power and status of the chiefs. Smith even appointed Ndiweni as a minister in the government in 1976 to convince the world of his interest in African welfare.

52. Cary and Mitchell, *op. cit.*, 7–12, 33–4.

53. Interviews with G. Chavunduka, 22 April 1976, J. J. Dube, 14 April 1976, J. Msika, 15 April 1976, G. Nyandoro, 12 May 1976. G. Kahari, however, in an interview on 21 April 1976, stated the opinion that tribalism was rife in African politics. In interviews with Bridget Bloom, broadcast on BBC Radio 4 in *Through African Eyes,* on 31 January and 7 February 1978, Mugabe, Nkomo, and Sithole stated that tribalism was not a major factor, but Muzorewa thought it was a problem.

54. *Zimbabwe Star,* 25 October 1975, spoke in its editorial about 'the evil' and 'the devil' of tribalism, of which the leaders of the Muzorewa ANC, it alleged, were guilty.

55. Dumbutshena, for example, tried to disparage Sithole by accusing him of appealing to the Shona in 1963 to reject Nkomo as a Ndebele and to form a political group according to tribal affiliation: E. Dumbutshena, *Zimbabwe Tragedy* (Nairobi, 1975), 42, 49.

56. Interviews with A. Chadzingwa, 30 April 1976, J. Chinamano, 25 April 1976, W. Musarurwa, 2 May 1976, C. C. Ngcebetsha, 15 April 1976.

57. Perhaps those who voted for Ndiweni's UNFP were motivated by fear of Muzorewa's imagined partiality for the Shona.

58. Ranger, 'Rhodesia's politics of tribalism', 496.

59. *The Herald,* 21 May 1959.

60. Cary and Mitchell, *op. cit.*, 41–4, 57–63.

61. *Ibid.,* 158.

62. *The Herald,* 10, 11 May 1979.

63. Ranger 'Rhodesia's politics of tribalism', 497.

The Impact of the War[1]

by

A. R. Wilkinson

INTRODUCTION

Even before Ian Smith unilaterally declared Rhodesia independent in November 1965 the then Labour Prime Minister, Harold Wilson, had already made it clear that he would not intervene militarily in the event of such action. Instead, the British Government initiated international economic sanctions which, as Wilson stated to the Commonwealth Prime Ministers' Conference at Lagos in January 1966, were expected to bring about the capitulation of the illegal regime within 'weeks rather than months'. It was left to the Zimbabwe nationalist movement to take up the military option. Both rival nationalist organisations, ZAPU and ZANU, determined to embark on a campaign of guerilla warfare rather than the somewhat haphazard and ineffectual acts of political violence which had occurred during the previous four years.

In the decade following UDI, however, the system of white supremacy in Rhodesia demonstrated resilience and determination in the face of such military, economic, and diplomatic pressures. The country's seizure of independence was vigorously and successfully asserted by all sections of the white-ruled state. The main effect of sanctions was to induce a considerable degree of self-sufficiency in the modern cash economy. Import substitution saw the mushrooming of the local manufacturing sector and a programme of diversification removed white agriculture's lop-sided dependence on tobacco production. Sanctions were half-heartedly applied and Rhodesian traders displayed considerable energy and ingenuity in evading them. By the early 1970s the Rhodesian economy had undergone a remarkable transformation—a performance which boosted the confidence of the Rhodesian Front government and the white community in general.

This self-confidence was apparent in the security field as well. Several offensives by black nationalist forces had been effectively contained. Their activities during the last half of the 1960s and the early 1970s never posed a really serious threat to the survival of the white minority regime but it did have the effect of increasing the size, experience, and expertise of the Rhodesian regular and reserve security forces which, after 1966, had been reorganised on a counter-insurgency basis.

While white Rhodesians enjoyed for the seven or eight years following UDI an almost exclusive monopoly of political, economic, and military power, black morale was correspondingly low. Confronted with these realities it was successive British Governments (Labour as well as Conservative), not the Rhodesian regime, which made the major concessions during the series of Anglo-Rhodesian constitutional negotiations over this period—i.e. the *Tiger* proposals in 1966, the *Fearless* terms in 1968, and the 1971 settlement. White Rhodesian politics drifted ineluctably in a rightward direction during this period. However, three events acted as catalysts in reversing the economic and military fortunes of the Rhodesian Front regime.

The first of these was the overwhelmingly negative verdict of the black community on the 1971 Anglo-Rhodesian Settlement, registered in May 1972 by the Pearce Commission whose task it had been to test the acceptability of these proposals to the population as a whole. This proved a major psychological turning point in black morale. There was a resurgence of armed resistance at the end of 1972 which continued and gathered momentum. The second event was Portugal's withdrawal from Africa following the April 1974 Lisbon coup. The appearance of a radical FRELIMO government in Mozambique had the dual effect of opening up Rhodesia's longest and most vulnerable border to insurgent infiltration and of closing off an important sanctions-busting route. The final factor contributing to the mounting pressures which increasingly threatened to undermine the continued viability of the Salisbury regime was the impact of the world economic recession following the energy crisis precipitated by the October 1973 Middle-East war. The Salisbury administration and its security forces were confronted with prosecuting an expanding war in increasingly straitened economic circumstances and in continued diplomatic isolation. The impact of the war can be assessed by referring to some of the critical indicators.

SOME CRITICAL INDICATORS

The territorial expansion of the fighting, which seriously stretched Rhodesian regular and reserve forces, is best illustrated by the dramatic improvement of the nationalist guerillas' position since the mid-sixties in terms of strategic geography (see map). Until 1971–72 Rhodesian security forces had to contend with nationalist guerilla infiltration from only one direction. This was the 750km border with Zambia which posed severe logistical and political problems for the guerillas. The Zambezi river and Lake Kariba were major inhibitions to large-scale infiltration. Even when crossed, the main targets of the guerillas remained a long way from the border and in the intervening space the local population was neither numerous nor sympathetic enough to sustain an effective guerilla offensive. The security forces also enjoyed the advantages of superior training and tactics, firepower and mobility as well as command of the air. Large concentrations of infiltrating guerillas were easily located and destroyed. The gradual disintegration of Portuguese control in the early 1970s throughout Mozambique's Tete province, however, enabled ZANU guerillas, with the assistance of the anti-Portuguese liberation movement, FRELIMO, to reopen the north-eastern front in parts of which ZAPU operatives had earlier been active. Here the guerillas were able to take advantage of a much more favourable socio-political

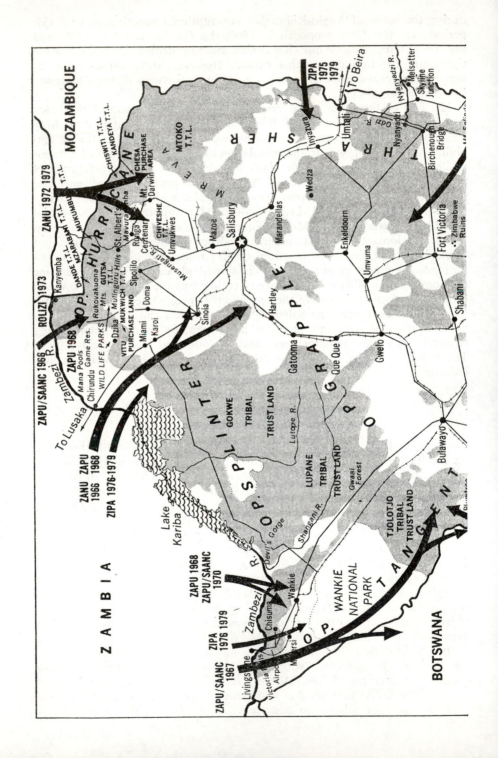

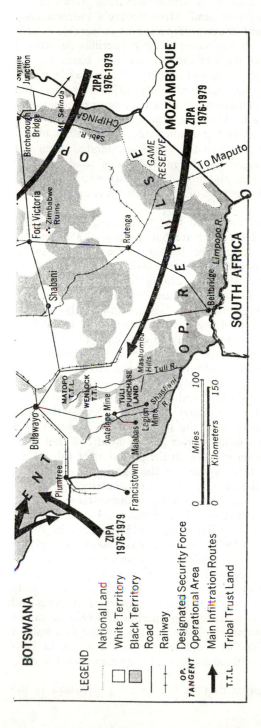

This map shows how, under the land-tenure system, the white population is concentrated on the Y-shaped central plateau which contains the main urban centres and lines of communication, while the majority of the black population is confined to the under-developed Tribal Trust Lands on the country's periphery. It illustrates how white-ruled Rhodesia has fallen a ready candidate for Mao Tse-tung's dictum of guerilla strategy that the cities should be surrounded from the countryside. The expansion of guerilla activities (indicated by incursion routes and Rhodesian security force operational zones) shows how this process of encirclement has developed during the years since 1966. In 1976 ZAPU's military wing, ZIPRA, and ZANU's military wing, ZANLA, were nominally integrated under the Zimbabwe People's Army, ZIPA.

This map has been reproduced from *Black Fire! Accounts of the Guerilla War in Rhodesia* by Michael Raeburn, with Introduction and Conclusion by Anthony R. Wilkinson (London, Julian Friedmann, 1978).

and physical terrain. Then, with Portugal's withdrawal from Africa in the wake of the April 1974 Lisbon coup and Mozambique's independence in June 1975, Rhodesia's longer and in every respect most vulnerable border was also exposed. Finally, from the beginning of 1976 guerillas penetrated deep into the southern and central areas of the country from bases in both Zambia and Mozambique. The presence and activity of guerillas in urban and semi-urban areas also increased markedly. By 1979, therefore, the security situation, partly by design and partly through accidents of geography and history, corresponded closely to Mao Tse-tung's strategic dictum that the cities should be surrounded from the countryside. The mainly black-inhabited Tribal Trust Lands, from which the guerillas operated, encircled the white-inhabited central plateau where the main lines of road and rail, nearly all the significant urban centres, and most of the white-owned farmland were located. By mid-1979 over 90 per cent of the country was under martial law.

In March 1976 it was officially estimated that there were 700 guerillas inside the country. By April 1977 the estimate had risen to 2,350, and by early 1979 it was thought that there were 10,000 in the six operational zones. In mid-1979 the figure was estimated at 13,000, rising to 15,000 by the end of November. Repeated official predictions about the war ending, or at least running down, proved ill-founded. In late 1973 the then Rhodesian Army Commander, Lieutenant-General Peter Walls, confidently claimed that the security forces were 'on top of the terrorist menace in as much as they had contained it and were now on the way to eradicating it'.[2] In 1974 the Minister of Justice, answering an MP who suggested the introduction of martial law, said that this 'would be admitting that the Government had lost control of that area... Martial law only comes into existence when the civil powers have lost control and they hand over to the army to maintain the law and order position of the country'.[3] More recently the Rev Ndabaningi Sithole predicted, shortly after the signing of the 3 March 1978 Internal Agreement, that the war would be over by the middle of that year. In fact the war entered its most intense phase in the period after July 1978.

Apart from this dramatic territorial spread of the fighting, its gathering intensity was also reflected by the rapidly mounting casualty figures. By the start of 1979 total casualties since the beginning of the sustained guerilla offensive at the end of 1972 amounted to: white civilians—310 (60 per cent of which occurred in 1978); black civilians—3845 (45 per cent in 1978); security forces—760 (37 per cent in 1978); and guerillas—6000+ (nearly 50 per cent in 1978). These figures are derived from security forces communiqués and almost certainly underestimate the numbers killed in all categories although they provide a reasonably credible guide to the intensity of the war. They do not, for example, include the numbers of guerillas and non-combatants killed in Rhodesian attacks on guerilla and refugee camps in neighbouring states. The momentum of the war during the first half of 1979 suggested that, if maintained or increased, it would result in 1979 claiming more deaths than the combined total of all the years since the early guerilla operations after UDI.

Another measure of the deterioration in the security situation is the substantial increase in defence and defence-related expenditure between the 1971–72 and 1977–78 budgets. The allocation to the Ministry of Defence rose by 610 per cent; the Police vote by 232 per cent; that of the Ministry of Internal Affairs by 305 per cent; and the Department of Roads and Road Traffic by 257 per cent. In July 1978, anticipating a de-escalation of the war after the 3 March Internal Agreement, the proportion of the budget allocated to the war was reduced by one per cent. This was the first reduction since 1972. The failure to reduce the level of conflict necessitated, however, a supplementary estimate in December 1978 of an additional seven per cent, which exceeded the initial reduction. With the war costing around $1 million a day there was no way in which the cost of the security burden could have been shouldered by the new state of Zimbabwe/Rhodesia on its own. A former Rhodesian Front Deputy Minister admitted as far back as late 1976 that South Africa had been subsidising Rhodesia's defence bill to the tune of fifty per cent.[4] The increasing burdens of the war since then meant still greater dependence.

In order to cover the rapid rise in security expenditure from local resources, taxation has been increased on several occasions over the past few years. This applied to both individual and company tax as well as indirect taxation. In addition, a National Defence Levy of 12.5 per cent was introduced in 1978, though this was removed in mid-1979. In September 1978 the journal of the Associated Chambers of Commerce of Rhodesia commented: 'The deeply unpopular National Defence Levy was in the circumstances just about the only measure the Treasury could adopt to boost government revenues. Already a third of total spending will be deficit financed, probably to the tune of Rh.$310 million. As it is, the revenue intake of the government is likely to be around 10 per cent lower than that achieved in the last tax year. This is due to the narrowing tax base caused by white emigration and declining company profits, but also by the effects of low consumer confidence on sales tax revenues.'[5]

Whereas there had been a steady growth in Gross Domestic Product up to 1974, there had since been a negative growth rate. In 1975 it was –1 per cent, in 1976 –3.5 per cent, and –7 per cent in 1977. According to the Rhodesian Banking Corporation (Rhobank), '1978 was, not unexpectedly, the fourth consecutive year of falling real output in the economy, bringing to 15 per cent the loss in total output since the start of the recession at the beginning of 1975 and to an alarming 25 per cent the erosion of real per capita incomes since the peak recorded in 1974. Surprisingly though, last year's decline in real Gross Domestic Product was restricted to an estimated 4 per cent, which compares very well indeed with the record 6.9 per cent fall recorded in 1977 and the official mid-year forecast of around 7 per cent. Even though this overall improvement was attributable more to the lower rate of inflation in 1978 than to any meaningful gains in the volume of output growth, the mere fact that the economy was able to hold its own in the face of so much adversity says a great deal for its inherent strength and resilience . . . Still there is no denying the fact that four years of economic stagnation, accompanied by a progressive deterioration in the internal political and security environment has seriously impaired the country's developmental process to the point where it will now take many years for it to recover lost ground.'[6] Without an end to, or at least a significant slackening of, the war the opportunity to recover lost ground by taking advantage of the economy's 'inherent strength and resilience' would be lost. Furthermore, the lower rate of inflation in 1978 was not maintained. Up to 1975 inflation had been kept well under control. Since then the problem became more acute and the events in Iran probably boosted inflation yet further.

The employment situation has deteriorated markedly over the past three years. Both white and black employment fell from their high points in 1975 back to 1973 levels. Whereas between 1969 and 1975 the economy had succeeded in absorbing almost all the 40,000 black school leavers entering the labour market annually, it later proved incapable of taking in the much larger number of school leavers—estimated at 70,000 annually.[7] The result was a rapidly accumulating backlog of unemployed and it was from their ranks that the guerilla armies drew many of their recruits.

The lack of white manpower assumed increasingly serious proportions. With a decline in the numbers of local Rhodesian whites, this traditionally important source of recruitment into the regular security forces proved less and less adequate. Consequently there was an increased reliance on alternative sources. In the late 1970s foreigners from North America, Western Europe, and Australasia were recruited. At its peak the number may have reached around 2,000 but, it is believed, this had probably fallen to about 500 by mid-1979.[8] The other main source of regular army recruitment was from the black population for the Rhodesian African Rifles. In 1972 there was just one white-officered RAR battalion of under 1,000 men. Under military and political pressures the number of men probably increased seven- or eight-fold and blacks were commissioned at the lower levels, RAR personnel being used to supplement under-strength Territorial battalions. Much of the security burden fell on the Territorials and National Service conscripts (who were previously non-blacks). Men between 18 and 38 were expected to spend up to half the year on operational duty away from their families and normal civilian occupations; those between 38 and 50 up to 70 days; and those over 50 up to 40 days with the Police Reserve. Clearly the withdrawal of so many people for such extended periods had a severely adverse effect on the economy. 'Make-up' pay, the differential between civilian and army earnings, had in addition to be paid by either the Army or the employers.

Tourism, an important earner of foreign exchange, was a major casualty of the war. As the following figures indicate, the slump in tourism between 1973 and 1978 related directly to the deterioration in the security situation. The number of holiday visitors to Rhodesia dropped by 74 per cent from a high point of 339,210 in 1972 (before the resurgence of the war) to a low of 87,943 in 1978. In 1973 the number was 243,812, in 1974 229,570, in 1975 244,404, in 1976 140,423, in 1977 103,515, in 1978 87,943.[9] The slight improvement in 1975 was probably attributable to the diversion of South African tourists from Mozambique as well as to the less intense guerilla activity inside Rhodesia during the *détente* negotiations and their aftermath. In September 1976 the Finance Minister announced cutbacks in holiday allowances for Rhodesians travelling abroad in an attempt to reduce the amount of money leaving the country and to help deter unofficial emigration (holiday allowances were used by intending emigrants as a means of getting additional funds out of the country). Official emigration allowances were also reduced and at the time the Minister estimated that these cuts together would save $40 million.[10] Holiday allowances were, however, subsequently eased a little. The new administration, in an apparently desperate attempt to halt mounting white emigration, announced plans to introduce a $20,000 're-entry' fee for anyone who emigrated but then decided to return.

Although the mining sector, a critical earner of foreign exchange, was able not only to sustain but even to improve its output value despite the war, the future is less reassuring. The Anglo-American Corporation ceased its prospecting operations. The Chairman of Rio Tinto also warned of the damage which would result to the industry if the war continued and the loss of skilled manpower continued: 'The new government can rest assured of our cooperation in overcoming this problem, but all our efforts will come to nothing if there is not a rapid de-escalation of the war.'[11]

The most important barometer of white morale, reflecting all these pressures, was the emigration rate. The migration patterns in 1978 and 1979 reflected this sensitivity to political developments. The total net negative migration was 13,709 in 1978 and reached 7,920 in the first nine months of 1979. Over the period 1960–79, 180,881 people entered the country while 202,950 departed. This turnover rate was roughly equivalent to three-quarters of the more or less quarter of a million whites living in Rhodesia during this period. In the first six months of 1978 the rate slackened appreciably, averaging only 613 departures a month compared with 960 in the corresponding period of 1977. The overall loss during the first half of 1977 was less than a third over the previous year's. This no doubt reflected the 'wait and see' attitude of whites towards the March 1978 Internal Agreement's capacity to bring about the lifting of sanctions, diplomatic recognition, and a cease-fire. None of these were achieved and the mood of cautious optimism apparent in the first half of 1978 rapidly evaporated. In the latter half of the year the average monthly net outflow at 1,672 was well above twice the average for the corresponding period of the previous year. The total net negative migration of 13,709 in 1978 was the highest in the country's history. After the resurgence of the guerilla war in 1973 the post-1966 trend of a positive inflow of immigrants was reversed. Having averaged an annual net inflow of 6,310 in the six years 1967–72, the decline in the subsequent six years was very marked. In 1973, 1974, and 1975 the figures were respectively 1,683, 1,599, and 1,925. The latter two years would certainly have registered negative figures had it not been for an abnormal influx of Portuguese settlers from Mozambique and Angola after the Lisbon coup. As the fighting widened and intensified from 1976 the outflow gathered momentum. In 1976 there was a net outflow of 7,072, in 1977 10,908. Nearly 13,000 more people (net) left Rhodesia from the beginning of 1976 to September 1979 than in the longer period 1960 to 1966 which was attended by the crises of the disintegration of the Central African Federation and UDI.

The qualitative aspect of this emigration is equally significant. It included large numbers of professional and skilled whites, whose qualifications and expertise enable them to compete for jobs abroad on equal terms. There is also, however, a substantial number of whites who, despite inadequate qualifications and skills, have nevertheless been able to enjoy in Rhodesia an artificially high standard of living which they could not hope to attain elsewhere. Many in this category would find difficulty in emigrating at a time when potential host countries have severe unemployment. This posed a serious problem for Bishop Muzorewa's Administration since it was precisely at the lower levels of employment that black pressure for advancement was greatest. On the other hand, the new regime faced likely collapse if the exodus of whites with professional qualifications and specialised skills, upon which the continued viability of the Administration depended, was not halted (see Table).

The Influence of Political and Security Developments on White Migration

	Immigrants	Emigrants	Net Flow (approx)	Contraventions of Law and Order (Maintenance) Act
1960	8,000	7,000	+ 1,000	no figures available
1961[a]	8,000	10,000	− 2,000	901
1962	8,000	12,000	− 4,000	1,112
1963	7,000	18,000	−11,000	961
1964	7,000	15,710	− 8,710	4,435
1965[b]	11,128	8,850	+ 2,278	2,319
1966	6,418	8,510	− 2,092	724
1967	9,618	7,570	+ 2,048	310
1968	11,864	5,650	+ 6,214	101
1969[c]	10,929	5,890	+ 5,039	57
1970	12,227	5,890	+ 6,337	130
1971	14,743	5,340	+ 9,403	396
1972[d]	13,966	5,150	+ 8,816	636
1973[e]	9,433	7,750	+ 1,683	
1974[f]	9,649	9,050	+ 599*	
1975	12,425	10,500	+ 1,925*	
1976[g]	7,782	14,854	− 7,072	
1977[h]	5,730	16,638	−10,908	
1978[i]	4,360	18,069	−13,709	
	178,272	192,421	−14,149	

Sources: *Monthly Migration and Tourist Statistics* (CSO, Salisbury); and *Annual Reports* of the Commissioner of the British South Africa Police.

* These would almost certainly have been negative had it not been for an estimated 20,000 Portuguese refugees from Angola and Mozambique after the Lisbon coup. In addition this figure may have been boosted by the ambitious but largely unsuccessful Settlers 74 immigration campaign.

a.   The early 1960s saw the disintegration of the Central African Federation and widespread political violence in urban and rural areas.

b.   UDI by Rhodesia in November. Several insurgent offensives during 1966, 1967 and
     1968 were successfully contained while sanctions failed to bring about economic
     collapse.
c.   No reported military activity by guerillas during the year.
d.   Apart from a few clashes with security forces in early 1970, there was no reported
     armed resistance until the end of 1972. In May 1972 the Pearce Commission registered
     an overwhelming black rejection of the November 1971 settlement proposals and
     there was a resurgence of guerilla activity at the end of the year.
e.   The guerilla war continued.
f.   Portugal's withdrawal from Africa after the April 1974 Lisbon coup was followed by
     the regional initiative on Rhodesia of South Africa and black front-line states, which
     had broken down by March 1976.
g.   The fighting widened and intensified from 1976 onwards. Mr Smith was forced to
     accept the 'Kissinger' terms for majority rule in two years in September. The subse-
     quent Geneva conference to negotiate the transition to majority rule collapsed in
     December while the war intensified and imposed severe economic and social strains
     on the white community.
h.   A new Anglo-American initiative was announced in April and the Anglo-American
     plan was revealed in September. There was no progress towards any all-party con-
     ference but an Internal Settlement between Smith, Muzorewa, Sithole and Chirau
     was signed on 3 March 1978. Hopes for recognition and the lifting of sanctions
     were disappointed.
i.   This year saw the highest proportion of casualties of any year for guerillas, the
     security forces, and black and white civilians. Predictions of a cease-fire by mid-1978
     did not materialise. The fighting intensified and the election was postponed until
     April. The whites approved the 1979 Constitution in the January referendum and
     Muzorewa won the internal election in April.

The physical and psychological strains and stresses of the situation have
also been reflected by the rise in 'social casualties'. Marital problems,
unwanted pregnancies, drug addiction, and alcoholism have all increased
significantly over the last few years among the country's declining white
population.[12] While the white community has suffered increasing disruption
and distress, the lot of the black population has been very much worse—
especially in the rural areas.

Normal administration and services in the Tribal Trust Lands have been
severely disrupted. According to a report in the (Rhodesia) *Herald* in
November 1978, 951 black primary schools had closed, leaving more than
230,000 children without schooling (about 25 per cent of the total) as a
result of the war. Thirty-five secondary schools and their 9,000 pupils had
been similarly affected. Over 2,000 teachers had lost their jobs. A spokesman
for the Ministry of Education warned of a potential disaster: 'There could
be a whole lost generation of children . . . as far as literacy is concerned. . . .
One major problem is that it may well prove enormously difficult (because
of the pressure on school places), even if the war situation clears up, for
those children now out of school to return to their classes.'[13] Even more
serious, health authorities fear that there will be a high incidence of mental
retardation among the present generation of children arising out of the
conditions of severe malnutrition and starvation prevalent in many rural
areas. Apart from the inevitable disruption to the production of food crops,
it has been security policy to deny or curtail food supplies to the Tribal
Trust Lands so as to prevent them falling into the hands of the guerillas.
In these circumstances the rural population have become highly vulnerable

to the resurgence of a variety of diseases at a time when medical services have either ceased to exist or operate on a much reduced basis.

The livestock population in the Tribal Trusts Land has also been drastically affected. As early as October 1977 an official was quoted as saying that 'There is absolutely nothing that can be done about it until the war ends and veterinary services are restored in the tribal areas'. Tsetse fly, screw worm, and a variety of tick-borne diseases, once well under control, have become widespread. By early 1979 it was reported that only 1,500 out of 8,000 cattle dips were still in operation. An estimated one-third of black-owned cattle in the Tribal Trust Lands has been lost and the diseases threaten to spill over into the 2.6 million cattle on white-owned farms.[14]

Tax collection has broken down in large parts of the security-affected rural areas and bus services were cut by fifty per cent, according to a report at the end of 1978.[15] Buses were particularly vulnerable to hold-ups and mines. Black private motorists, for whom travelling was once fairly safe from guerilla ambushes, are reported to have joined convoy traffic in increasing numbers. Life for many non-combatant tribespeople has become intolerable, caught as they are between the demands of the security forces (including the 'auxiliary' followers of Muzorewa and Sithole), on the one hand, and guerilla forces of the two wings of the Patriotic Front, on the other. As one of the very few organisations with access to these areas and with no political axe to grind, the International Red Cross issued an appeal to all parties condemning the mounting horror of a war which was being waged by both sides with increasing brutality and disregard for human life.[16] The main result of such disruption in the rural areas is a massive refugee problem with drifts not only into neighbouring countries but also into the main urban centres.

CONCLUSION

There is no doubt that the mounting internal and external pressures generated by the war since 1973 have been primarily responsible for moving a reluctant Rhodesian Front regime away from the policies of almost undiluted white supremacy which it had pursued with so much determination after unilaterally declaring Rhodesia independent in 1965. The years of increasingly savage and bitter fighting which occurred after UDI inevitably inflicted deep physical and psychological wounds on the country and its peoples. Even if peace is established and the wounds healed, the scars will be evident for a decade and longer. Whatever government finally emerges in an independent Zimbabwe, whether or not a political settlement is successfully implemented, will be confronted by problems of reconciliation and reconstruction of awesome proportions.

A primary task will be facilitating the adjustment of individuals and groups in a deeply divided society, which has grown accustomed to the brutalising influences of the war, to the conditions necessary for the re-establishment of peace and a return to normality. The magnitude of the challenge is illustrated by the fact that at the end of 1979 there were up to

150,000 individuals with varying degrees of military training and experience, with access to arms, and owing allegiance to several established political organisations and party leaders. These included the white-controlled Rhodesian Army and Police comprising regular as well as reserve personnel; the private armies of Bishop Muzorewa's UANC and Mr Sithole's ZANU which have been integrated as 'auxiliaries' under the Zimbabwe Rhodesian Army; and the two military wings of the Patriotic Front, ZIPRA and ZANLA.

With a high degree of motivation and considerable experience behind it, the Rhodesian Army won a reputation for being a proficient but ruthless anti-insurgent force although, as the official casualty statistics themselves suggest, very often little effort was made to discriminate between guerillas and non-combatant civilians. The worst offenders, it would seem from the cases which have come to public notice, tend to have been in the para-military and reservist units which lacked the same degree of regular army discipline (e.g. the Guard Force, the Home Affairs Force, the Auxiliary Force, the Selous Scouts and Grey Scouts, and Police and Army reservists). The problem was particularly serious with respect to the Auxiliary Force which, although under the nominal control of the Army, was in general poorly trained and ill-disciplined. The Auxiliary Force, known as *Pfumo revanhu* (Spear of the People) was supported by teenage recruits called *Ziso revanhu* (Eyes of the People), who acted as informers.

The situation is equally complex and dangerous on the guerilla side as a report by the Catholic Commission for Justice and Peace in Rhodesia noted:

> Although it is not possible to give a comprehensive picture, it appears that there are two distinct types of guerilla groups operating in the country at present. One type is well trained, well disciplined and maintains the trust of the people. Another however, is poorly trained and ill-disciplined and can only maintain the allegiance of the rural population through the use of terror tactics.[17]

The guerillas are also supported by para-military groups of young people known as *mujibas* whose function was similar to Bishop Muzorewa's *Ziso revanhu*. The report refers to the further complicating factor that:

> In addition to the guerilla and government-related forces there are independent bandit groups who owe allegiance to no one; some are former guerillas who have set up on their own, others are groups who were former auxiliaries and still other small groups of what one can only call criminals and who have never been members of any formal command structure.

In these circumstances there are clearly great dangers not only for any pre-election cease-fire, but also for the period immediately after independence.

On the guerilla side there will almost certainly be individuals and groups who will simply secrete their weapons and merge into the local population. Equally, on the other side, it will be difficult, if not impossible, to ensure adequate control over thousands of civilians holding personal arms. The same problem applies to some army units, such as the Auxiliary Force, and the Selous Scouts whose members have arms caches deposited throughout the country. There is, therefore, in the absence of any substantial external peace-keeping force, a risk of localised breaches of a cease-fire by dissident guerillas (or bandit groups masquerading as guerillas) as well as spontaneous revolts by white civilians (some of whom have threatened to assassinate Patriotic Front leaders in revenge for those who died in the Viscounts shot down by guerilla forces) as occurred, for instance, during the transition to independence in Algeria and Mozambique. Furthermore, in the absence of any agreement on integrating the rival armies into a post-independence Zimbabwe Army, there is the risk that one side or the other will attempt to reverse an adverse election result by force. Such a development would run a real danger of internationalising the civil war which has already assumed serious regional dimensions.

In addition to these immediate/short-term and essentially military dangers, there are the medium/longer-term socio-economic problems for Zimbabwe's future security and stability. The return of large numbers of guerillas and refugees will impose an immense extra burden on an already critical unemployment situation, especially in the urban areas. These have already had their resources strained to the limit by the massive demographic upheaval caused by the war. The priority task of re-settling and rehabilitating the vast numbers of people displaced and dispossessed by the fighting will inevitably aggravate what has always been the most sensitive issue underlying racial conflict in Rhodesia—land. Superimposed on all this is the worrying resurgence of tribal divisions within the Black population reflected by the appearance of tribally-based political parties. It is certainly true that the Patriotic Front's willingness to negotiate a compromise settlement owed much to the persuasion of the Front Line States whose own serious economic and security problems had been aggravated by the Rhodesian war. However, if any collapse of a settlement leads to South African intervention, the Front Line States would probably have nowhere else to turn but to the socialist and communist countries.

NOTES

1. This article on Rhodesia/Zimbabwe is based on material from a wider unpublished research project on Southern Africa funded by the Rockefeller Foundation and undertaken by the author while a Research Associate at the International Institute for Strategic Studies, to both of which he wishes to express his gratitude.
2. *The Times,* 23 October 1973.
3. Rhodesian House of Assembly, *Parliamentary Debates,* 1974, vol 88, col 595.
4. *The Financial Times,* 1 November 1976, quoting an extract from a speech to a closed Rhodesian Front meeting by the then Deputy Minister in the Prime Minister's Office, Ted Sutton-Pryce.
5. *Commerce,* September 1978. (The Defence Levy was removed in the July 1979 budget.)
6. *Rhobank Economic Bulletin,* January 1979.
7. *Ibid.*
8. Personal communication from security force source.
9. *Monthly Migration and Tourist Statistics,* Central Statistical Office, Salisbury, Rhodesia.
10. *The Financial Times,* 26 July 1976.

11. *The Herald,* 10 May 1979.
12. *Ibid.,* 23 October 1978.
13. *Ibid.,* 22 November 1978.
14. *Ibid.,* 17 October 1977, and *New African,* April 1979.
15. *The Herald,* 17 October 1977.
16. Reported in *The Sunday Mail* (Rhodesia), 19 November 1978.
17. *Rhodesia at War: A Story of Mounting Suffering* (Salisbury, Catholic Commission for Justice and Peace, September 1979).